SELECTED POEMS OF T. A. DALY

Selected Poems

OF

T. A. DALY

including songs from

McARONI BALLADS

CANZONI & SONGS OF WEDLOCK

MADRIGALI

CARMINA

McARONI MEDLEYS

With an introductory letter by

CHRISTOPHER MORLEY

HARCOURT, BRACE AND COMPANY

NEW YORK

Typography by Robert Josephy
PRINTED IN THE UNITED STATES OF AMERICA
BY QUINN & BODEN COMPANY, INC., RAHWAY, N. J.

To Herself and the Houseful

A Letter to the Publishers

You ask me what is almost impossible when you ask a word
of preface for what needs none. In the first place, my own asso-
ciations with Tom Daly are so intricate with affection and feeling of all sorts that they have become very definitely our own
affair. Then (he will deny this) Mr. Daly has so vividly the
specialized sensitiveness of the poet and the leprechaun that to
pay homage in the wrong tone of voice will be offensive. And
third, his poems, loved by many thousands, long since won their
way into all hearts. Among verse that has become really "pop-
ular" they are almost unique for polished accuracy of form and
cadence. It is now thirty years since that first little edition of
Canzoni was issued in Philadelphia. And it is graceless indeed
to write in professional mood of one who seems like an older
brother. One's friends are for love; not for analysis.

I once inherited Tom Daly's old rolltop desk in the office of
the Philadelphia *Evening Public Ledger*. With that desk perhaps I inherited also an inside glimpse of his ardors and endu-
rances. There was a lot of dusty old copy-paper in it, and a large
bottle of ink, which I remember was oddly labeled *Commercial
Fluid* (a term which seems to have gone out of use in the ink
business). I can't believe that Tom willingly used ink from a
bottle with that legend. Irish by inheritance, poet by nature, there
is no drop of commercial fluid in his veins. I think rather of a
ridiculous story of some newspaper publishers' dinner held many
years ago at the old Waldorf in New York. Tom was present in
his official capacity as general manager of a religious paper. At
his particular table conviviality went its circling round, and presently it was his turn to buy. Nothing but the best was ever too
good for Tom, and with the enthusiasm of a Philadelphian in
the Big Town for an evening he commanded champagne. But
imagine his delight when a table companion, exhilarated beyond
restraint, sprang up and called the whole banquet-hall to atten-

tion. "Gentlemen," he cried, "I give you the health of the *Catholic Standard and Times* of Philadelphia; the only religious paper buying wine tonight."

It is not commercial fluid, but pure wine, that Tom Daly has always poured for his readers. The vintage wine of true and deep sentiment, of kindly humor and most moving pathos. Surely it was some fine instinct in him that led him, in his verses that are best known, to serve as spokesman for those least able to express themselves.

When I first got to know Tom well (he was my father confessor when I began newspaper work) I used to notice his hands. We lunched together several times a week for three years, and either eating or drinking, telling stories or rolling cigarettes, those sinewy members were frequently visible. One of his fingers was oddly crooked; kinked by a baseball when he played shortstop for Fordham many years ago. And it occurred to me that in his art of writing was just the same unexpected twist. Those who know him, whether on paper or in his matchless moods of narrative, recognize the instinctive and unsurpassed story-teller; who understands by unerring intuition how to suspend, withhold, misleadingly divulge, and then finally clinch in triplicated surprise, the intended jape. Not only a great actor, but perhaps a great short-story writer, went missing when Tom Daly gave his prime gusto to the arts of verse. That he is adept in character suggestion his Italianate verses delightfully show. Gradually we find the various people—Giuseppe the barber, Padre Angelo, the muscular Carlotta, Antonio Sarto the mason, not merely identities in separate poems but living differentiated characters in a running plot. Only once, perhaps, did his cunning fail to carry the story through to its final perfected stroke. That was in the problem whether the hero should marry the beautiful Angela, or Carlotta who was "strong for carry wood." It was a shrewd small girl who solved it. "Of course," she said, "let him marry Angela, and he can hire Carlotta to work for them." *

* See "Between Two Loves" and "Da Wisa Child."

viii

Do I have to admit my own personal favorite among the dialect poems? I think it will have to be "The Blossomy Barrow"; not only because it is so unconsciously characteristic of the author himself, but also because last summer I had occasion to hire just such an Antonio Sarto. He was building a chimney for me, and was so intent on making it beautiful—according to his own gaudy ideas of masonry—that in matters of draught and heat radiation it is hopelessly inadequate. But what Etruscan patterns in stone!

I am glad that our poet has here made judicious assortment among the well-known pieces in dialect and the less familiar stanzas of English pure. Few writers have ever exposed with more winning frankness certain private and household emotions. "To a Thrush," that noble and beautiful expression of love in sorrow, stands at the top of this mood, and there are many others. These are for the sensitive to find, not for any outside hand to indicate.

"Daly the troubadour" Franklin P. Adams has called him, adapting the old line. ("Gaily the troubadour touched his guitar.") What is a troubadour exactly? Someone who finds things, I suppose. He has found good music in very simple hearts, and flowers growing round the heavy wheelbarrow of journalism. I remember once, hunting for something else in the morgue of the old *Evening Ledger,* I happened to come on the fat envelope of material for Tom's own obit, carefully put away (as is the habit of newspaper files) for eventuality. I borrowed it and Tom and I had a humorous lunch together rewriting it up to what we deemed his due. This pleased us, as Tom had lately been fired from that paper and I expected to be at any minute.

It's a grand obit, as I remember it; but I pray that it'll be a long time before it's needed.

CHRISTOPHER MORLEY

Contents

ITALICE

xi

HIBERNICE

A LA FRANCAISE

ANGLICE

SONGS OF THE MONTHS

Proem

TO A CORRESPONDENT

My favorite poet? I'm afraid
  You'll sneer at my selection;
And if "a poet's born, not made,"
  It may deserve rejection.
My poet's puny stature shows
  The lines that he is built on
Much less heroic are than those
  That moulded
               Milton.

'Tis true you may with *Byron's* fame
  Crush my poor bard's to jelly,
Or dim his rush-light in the flame
  That wreathes the name of
               Shelley.

Behold him, too, in thought or style
  Not even *Burns'* or *Blake's* peer—
Poor pigmy piping many a mile
  In rear of
            Shakespeare.

Yet not for any one of these
  Great names that loom above him
Would I exchange those qualities
  That make me fondly love him.
I love his living heart that sings
  And makes my blood flow faster;
I love so many little things
  Of which he is the master.

I love his ardent joy of life,
  And, faith—as I'm a sinner—
I love his bairns, his home, his wife,
  His appetite for dinner.
My favorite poet? I'll rejoice
  And tread this old earth gaily
As long as I can hear the voice
  Of

                              T. A. Daly

ITALICE

Da Comica Man

Giacobbe Finelli so funny, O! My!
By tweestin' hees face an' by weenkin' hees eye
He maka you laugh teell you theenk you weell die.
  He don't gotta say som'theeng; all he ees do
    Ees maka da face an', how moocha you try,
  You no can help laugh w'en he lookin' at you—
    Giacobbe Finelli so funny, O! My!

I deeg een da tranch weeth Giacobbe wan day;
Giacobbe ees toss up da spadefulla clay,
An' beeg Irish boss he ees gat een da way!
  Da boss he ees look at Giacobbe an' swear
    So bad as he can, but Giacobbe, so sly,
  He maka pretand he no see he was dere—
    Giacobbe Finelli so funny, O! My!

But w'en da boss turn an' ees starta for go,
Giacobbe look up an' he mak' da face—So!
I laugh an' I laugh lika deesa—Ho! ho!
  Da boss he com' back an' he poncha my head,
    He smasha my nose an' he blacka my eye—
  I no can help laugh eef I gona be dead.
    Giacobbe Finelli so funny, O! My!

Two 'Mericana Men

Beeg Irish cop dat walk hees beat
    By dees peanutta stan',
First two, t'ree week w'en we are meet
    Ees call me "Dagoman."
An' w'en he see how mad I gat,
    Wheech eesa pleass heem, too,
Wan day he say: "W'at's matter dat,
    Ain't 'Dago' name for you?
Dat's 'Mericana name, you know,
    For man from Eetaly;
Eet ees no harm for call you so,
    Den why be mad weeth me?"
First time he talka deesa way
    I am too mad for speak,
But nexta time I justa say:
    "All righta Meester Meeck!"

O! my, I nevva hear bayfore
    Sooch langwadge like he say;
An' he don't look at me no more
    For mebbe two, t'ree day.
But pretta soon agen I see
    Dees beeg poleecaman
Dat com' an' growl an' say to me;
    "Hallo, Eyetalian!
Now, mebbe so you gon' deny
    Dat dat'sa name for you."
I smila back an' mak' reply:
    "No, Irish, dat'sa true."
"Ha! Joe," he cry, "you theenk dat we
    Should call you 'Merican?"

"Dat's gooda 'nough," I say, "for me,
　　Eef dat's w'at you are, Dan."

So now all times we speaka so
　　Like gooda 'Merican:
He say to me, "Good morna, Joe,"
　　I say, "Good morna, Dan."

Mia Carlotta

Giuseppe, da barber, ees greata for "mash,"
He gotta da bigga, da blacka moustache,
Good clo'es an' good styla an' playnta good cash.

W'enevra Giuseppe ees walk on da street,
Da peopla dey talka, "how nobby! how neat!
How softa da handa, how smalla da feet."

He leefta hees hat an' he shaka hees curls,
An' smila weeth teetha so shiny like pearls;
Oh, manny da heart of da seelly young girls
       He gotta.
          Yes, playnta he gotta—
            But notta
            Carlotta!

Giuseppe, da barber, he maka da eye,
An' lika da steam engine puffa an' sigh,
For catcha Carlotta w'en she ees go by.

Carlotta she walka weeth nose in da air,
An' look through Giuseppe weeth far-away stare,
As eef she no see dere ees som'body dere.

Giuseppe, da barber, he gotta da cash,
He gotta da clo'es an' da bigga moustache,
He gotta da seelly young girls for da "mash,"
          But notta—
           You bat my life, notta—
            Carlotta.
            I gotta!

Da Sweeta Soil

All weenter-time I work for deeg
    Da tranch een ceety street,
An' I am looka like da peeg
    An' smal jus' 'bout as sweet,
Baycause my han's, my face, my clo'es
    Ees dirty as can be,
An' sewer-gas ees een my nose
    An' steeck all ovra me.
More dirty an' more mean I feel
    Dan I am look to you;
My soul eenside ees seeck, but steell,
    W'at am I gona do?
Ees notheeng sweet een ceety street
    For mak' me better man.
All men an' theengs dat I am meet
    Mak' meanness all dey can,
An' all dey speak ees ogly words
    An' do som' ogly theeng.
So even, too, dose leetla birds,
    Dat ought be glad an' seeng,
Dey fight each other een da dirt
    For dirty food dey eat.
Ah! so my soul eenside ees hurt
    For work een ceety street.

But yestaday! oh, yestaday,
    I leeve, I breathe again!
Da boss ees sand me far away
    For work een countra lane.
How can I mak' you ondrastand—
    You are so grand, so reech—

7

To know da joy I feel, my frand,
   For deeg dees countra deetch?
I sweeng my peeck, an' oh! da smal,
   W'en first I turn da sod!
So sweet! Escuse me eef I tal
   Ees like da breath of God.
So pure da soil, like Eetaly,
   I stoop an' taka piece
An' den—oh! don'ta laugh at me—
   I talk to eet and keess!
An' while I do dees foola theeng
   An' mak' so seelly tears,
Ees com' a pritta bird an' seeng
   Hees music een my ears.
You know dees 'Mericana bird,
   Weeth breast so lika flame,
So red; I do not know da word
   You say for call hees name,
But w'at he seeng ees plain to me,
   An' dees ees part of eet:
"Ees spreeng, ees spreeng een Eetaly,
   So sweeta, sweeta, sweet!"

Oh, eef you weesh da Dagoman,
   Dat com' for leeve weeth you,
To be da gooda 'Merican
   An' love dees countra, too,
I ask you tak' heem by da hand,
   Away from ceety street,
An' show heem first dees granda land
   Where eet ees pure an' sweet.

8

Da Leetla Boy

Da spreeng ees com'; but oh, da joy
    Eet ees too late!
He was so cold, my leetla boy,
    He no could wait.

I no can count how manny week,
How manny day, dat he ees seeck;
How manny night I seet an' hold
Da leetla hand dat was so cold.
He was so patience, oh, so sweet!
Eet hurts my throat for theenk of eet;
An' all he evra ask ees w'en
Ees gona com' da spreeng agen.
Wan day, wan brighta sunny day,
He see, across da alleyway,
Da leetla girl dat's livin' dere
Ees raise her window for da air,
An' put outside a leetla pot
Of—w'at-you-call?—forgat-me-not.
So smalla flower, so leetla theeng!
But steell eet mak' hees hearta seeng:
"Oh, now, at las', ees com' da spreeng!
Da leetla plant ees glad for know
Da sun ees com' for mak' eet grow.
So, too, I am grow warm and strong."
So lika dat he seeng hees song.
But, ah! da night com' down an' den
Da weenter ees sneak back agen,
An' een da alley all da night
Ees fall da snow, so cold, so white,
An' cover up da leetla pot
Of—w'at-you-call?—forgat-me-not.

9

All night da leetla hand I hold
Ees grow so cold, so cold, so cold!

Da spreeng ees com'; but oh, da joy
    Eet ees too late!
He was so cold, my leetla boy,
    He no could wait.

Between Two Loves

I gotta love for Angela,
  I love Carlotta, too.
I no can marry both o' dem,
  So w'at I gona do?

Oh, Angela ees pretta girl,
She gotta hair so black, so curl,
An' teeth so white as anytheeng.
An' oh, she gotta voice to seeng,
Dat mak' your hearta feel eet must
Jomp up an' dance or eet weell bust.
An' alla time she seeng, her eyes
Dey smila like Italia's skies,
An' makin' flirtin' looks at you—
But dat ees all w'at she can do.

Carlotta ees no gotta song,
But she ees twice so big an' strong
As Angela, an' she no look
So beautiful—but she can cook.
You oughta see her carry wood!
I tal you w'at, eet do you good.
W'en she ees be som'body's wife
She worka hard, you bat my life!
She nevva gattin' tired, too—
But dat ees all w'at she can do.

Oh, my! I weesh dat Angela
  Was strong for carry wood,
Or else Carlotta gotta song
  An' looka pretta good.

I gotta love for Angela,
  I love Carlotta, too.
I no can marry both o' dem,
  So w'at I gona do?

Da Wisa Child

All right, I know. All right, signor;
Da same old question like bayfore!
But you are not da only frand
Dat com' to dees peanutta stand
An' look me een da eye an' say:
"Com'! why you no gat married, eh?"
Today com' wan more wise dan you,
Dat mebbe gona help me, too.
Do you remembra long ago,
W'en first you speaka to me so,
How dat I mak' confess' to you
Dere was two fina girls I knew,
But dat I like dem both so wal
Eet was too hard for me to tal
Wheech wan be besta wife for me?
Wan girl was Angela, and she
Was jus' so pretta as can be;
An' she could seeng so sweet eet mak'
Your hearta jomp so like eet br'ak,
But dat was all dat she could do.
An' den dere was Carlotta, too,
Dat was da verra besta cook,
But had no song or pretta look
Like Angela, but steell was good
For keep da house and carry wood.
An' I was sad dat time, baycause
I want a wife, but steell da laws
Dey would not lat me marry two—
So w'at da deuce I gona do?
An' you—you had no word to say;
But here to me ees com' today
A leetla girl, good frand o' mine,

Dat's only eight year old, or nine,
But verra mooch more wise dan you.
An' w'at you s'pose she tal me do?
"Tak' Angela!" she say. "Why not?
Den both of you could pay Carlot'
To carry wood and cooka too,
An' justa keep da house for you."

Padre Domineec

Padre Domineec McCann
He ees great beeg Irish man.
   He ees growla w'en he speak,
Like he gona go for you
Jus' for busta you in two.
   My! he talk so rough, so queeck,
You weell weesha you could be
Som'where elsa w'en you see
   Padre Domineec.

Padre Domineec McCann
Stop at dees peanutta-stan'
   W'en my leetla boy ees seeck;
Talk so rough he mak' me cry,
Say ees besta boy should die
   So he go to Heaven queeck!
He ees speak so cold to me
Nevva more I wanta see
   Padre Domineec.

Den gran' doctor com'. Ees queer!
W'en I ask who sand heem here,
   He jus' smile an' weell no speak
Only justa for to say:
"You no gotta cent to pay,
   I gon' feex dees boy dat's seeck."
   .   .   .   .   .

O beeg-hearta man, an' true!
I am gattin' on to you,
   Padre Domineec!

The Audience

I mak' not moocha mon' today,
So few ees hear da tunes I play.
Long time bayfore da sun ees shine
I tak' dees street pian' of mine
An' pull eet out from ceety street
To countra lane, where cool an' sweet
Da morneeng breeza blow, an' where
All theengs ees beautiful an' fair.
Oh, here, I theenk, I gona find
Som' peopla so good-heart' an' kind
Dey weell be glad for hear me play
An' notta tal me "gona 'way!"
Lika mosta do dat I am meet
W'en I am play een ceety street.
I walk an' walk, but eet ees queer
I meet so few da peopla here;
Ees only wan or two, but steell
I look for more. I climb da heell
An' travel down da hotta road.
Da street pian' ees heavy load;
I am baygeen for feel da heat,
An' so, bimeby, I stop an' seet
Een shady place bayside da way.
Oh, I am mad! I growl an' say:
"I mak' not moocha mon' today.
W'at for you com', O! foola man!
Where no wan hear your street pian'?"
But, den, w'at s'pose ees happen me?
Firs' theeng you know, ees leetla tree
Mak' funny noisa where eet stan's,
So like as eef eet clap eets han's!
Den gentla feengers een da air

Dey com' an' pull me by da hair;
Ees som'theeng een dees sweeta breeze
Dat speak to me an' coax an' tease.
An' den da sky, so wide, so blue,
Eet seem to smile an' coax me, too.
So all theengs speak, as eef dey say:
"Com', let us have da music. Play!"
I play wan tune—yes, two, t'ree more—
Like w'at I nevva do bayfore!
I stop. Da sky cry: "More!" An' den
I play dem evra wan agen.
So, too, I leeft my voice an' seeng.
Da breeze say "More!" to evratheeng.
So all day long ees lika dat.
O! 'Mericana man, I gat
Som' curses an' som' food to eat,
W'en I am play een ceety street,
But here da sky, da breeze, da tree,
Dey speak Eetalian to me!

I mak' not moocha mon' today,
So few ees hear da tunes I play,
But where is reecher man dan I
Dat play to breeze, an' tree, an' sky?

Leetla Giorgio Washeenton

You know w'at for ees school keep out
    Dees holiday, my son?
Wal, den, I gona tal you 'bout
    Dees Giorgio Washeenton.

Wal, Giorgio was leetla keed
    Ees leeve long time ago,
An' he gon' school for learn to read
    An' write hees nam', you know.
He moocha like for gona school
    An' learna hard all day,
Baycause he no gat time for fool
    Weeth bada keeds an' play.
Wal, wan cold day w'en Giorgio
    Ees steell so vera small,
He start from home, but he ees no
    Show up een school at all!
Oh, my! hees Pop ees gatta mad
    An' so he tal hees wife:
"Som' leetla boy ees gon' feel bad
    Today, you bat my life!"
An' den he grab a bigga steeck
    An' gon' out een da snow
An' lookin' all aroun' for seek
    Da leetla Giorgio.
Ha! w'at you theenk? Firs' theeng he see
    Where leetla boy he stan',
All tangla up een cherry tree,
    Weeth hatchet een hees han'.
"Ha! w'at you do?" hees Pop he say,
    "W'at for you busta rule

An' stay away like dees for play
    Eenstead for gon' to school?"
Da boy ees say: "I no can lie,
    An' so I speaka true.
I stay away from school for try
    An' gat som' wood for you.
I theenka deesa cherry tree
    Ees gooda size for chop,
An' so I cut heem down, you see,
    For justa help my Pop."
Hees Pop he no can gatta mad,
    But looka please' an' say:
"My leetla boy, I am so glad
    You taka holiday."

Ees good for leetla boy, you see,
    For be so bright an' try
For help hees Pop; so den he be
    A granda man bimeby.
So now you gotta holiday
    An' eet ees good, you know,
For you gon' do da sama way
    Like leetla Giorgio.
Don't play so mooch, but justa stop,
    Eef you want be som' good,
An' try for help your poor old Pop
    By carry home som' wood;
An' mebbe so like Giorgio
    You grow for be so great
You gona be da Presidant
    Of dese Unita State'.

Where's Mussolini Gona Gat?

You aska me dat I should tal
  "Where's Mussolini gona gat?"
All right, I weell som' day—but, wal,
  I ain'ta justa ready yat.

Eh? W'at? You theenk I am too scare'
For geeve my answer, fair an' square,
Baycause he's lees'nin' ovra dere?
Ah, no, my frand, dat's justa lie;
An' so, for dat, I gona try
For geeve you now true reason why:
You see, w'en I am yo'nga man,
Bayfore I tak' dees fruita stan',
I use' for work weeth peeck an' spade
For learn da beeg contracta trade,
An' soon, I think, of all da treecks
Dat can be done weeth spades an' peecks,
An' weeth da blasta-powder, too,
Dere's notta wan I no can do!
Wal—maka shorta story long—
For all I am so smart an' strong,
Ees com' a day w'en all go wrong,
An' evratheeng ees standa steell.
We're deeggin' tonnel een a heell,
W'en, all for sodden, we are block'
By bigga bonch da granite rock.
We ain'ta count on dat, you know,
But steell we work, but, oh, so slow!
Den speaks a fallow, name ees Joe:
"Hi! geeve me room an' dynamite!"
Oh, my! da way he use da stuff,
So queeck, so planty, an' so rough!

He put som' here, he put som' dere,
An'—bang!—he justa don'ta care!
"Com' on!" he say, "we gat som'where!" . . .
Da gang an' me, we are so scare'
We run like sheeps for uppa-stair.
I heet so fast da backa-track
I busta muscles een my back.
An' last I hear dees Joe, he yal:
"All right! I do da job mysal'!" . . .
An' den, da firsta theeng you know,
On othra side da heell ees Joe!
Wal, dat'sa longa time ago;
An' now he's beeg contracta boss,
An' me? I'm justa total loss—

Eh? W'at? You ask me steell to tal
   "Where's Mussolini gona gat?"
All right, I say, som' day—but, hal!
   He ain'ta feenish blastin' yat.

July, 1925

21

Da Boy from Rome

Today ees com' from Eetaly
  A boy ees leeve een Rome,
An' he ees stop an' speak weeth me—
  I weesh he stay at home.

He stop an' say "Hallo," to me,
  An' w'en he standin' dere
I smal da smal of Eetaly
  Steell steeckin' een hees hair,
Dat com' weeth heem across da sea,
  An' een da clo'es he wear.

Da peopla bomp heem een da street,
  Da noise ees scare heem, too;
He ees so clumsy een da feet
  He don't know w'at to do,
Dere ees so many theeng he meet
  Dat ees so strange, so new.

He sheever an' he ask eef here
  Eet ees so always cold.
Den een hees eye ees com' a tear—
  He ees no vera old—
An', oh, hees voice ees soun' so queer
  I have no heart for scold.

He look up een da sky so gray,
  But oh, hees eye ees be
So far away, so far away,
  An' w'at he see I see.
Da sky eet ees no gray today
  At home een Eetaly.

He see da gladda peopla seet
　　Where warma shine da sky—
Oh, while he eesa look at eet
　　He ees baygeen to cry.
Eef I no growl an' swear a beet
　　So, too, my frand, would I.

Oh, why he stop an' speak weeth me,
　　Dees boy dat leeve een Rome,
An' com' today from Eetaly?
　　I weesh he stay at home.

Da Pup een da Snow

Deed you evra see Joy
  Gona wild weeth delight,
Jus' so lika small boy
W'en som' brighta new toy
  Mak's heem crazy excite'?
You would know w'at I mean
Eef you jus' coulda seen—
  Not so long time ago—
How my leetla fat pup
  Ees first play een da snow.

O! I scream an' I roar
  An' so shaka weeth laughtra,
Dat my sides dey are sore
  For mos' three-four days aftra.
An' how mooch I would try,
  I no speak weeth sooch skeell
I could put een your eye
  W'at ees fresh een mine steell:
How dat leetla pup romp
  All aroun' da whole place,
How he bark, how he jomp
  An' fall down on hees face;
How he fight, how he bite
  An' ees tumble aroun',
Teell hees cover' weeth white
  Lik a leetla fat clown;
W'at su'prise fill hees eyes
  W'en he see da flakes sail,
How he bark at da skies,
  How he chasa hees tail.

24

O! I weesh I could show
　　How ees looka, dat pup,
How he puff an' he blow
W'en hees leecked by da snow
　　An' ees gotta geeve up.
An' I sposa, no doubt,
　　You would say I am fibbin'
W'en I say hees tongue's out
　　Lika yarda peenk ribbon—
O! how mooch I would try,
　　I no speak weeth sooch skeell
I could put een your eye
　　W'at's so fresh een mine steell.
But I weesh you had been
Where you, too, coulda seen
　　W'at delighta me so—
How my leetla fat pup
　　Ees first play een da snow!

Da Posta-Card from Napoli

So, you gon' sail for Italy?
Ah, fine!—W'at can you do for me?
Oh, notheeng, please; I don'ta care—
I weesh you joy while you are dere,
An' I'll be glad for see you w'en
Da sheep ees breeng you home agen—
Eh? No! Oh, please don't sand to me
No peecture-card from Napoli!

Oh, yes, wan time da letter-man
Breeng soocha card to deesa stan';
Eet was from gentleman like you
Dat wanted to be kinda, too.
Eet showed da town, da bay—but, oh,
I deed not need; so wal I know!
Ah! no, please don'ta sand to me
No peecture-card from Napoli.

Oh, wal, Signor, you are so kind,
So good to me, I would no mind
Eef you would send me wan from Rome.
Eh? Rome? No, dat ees not my home.
Deed I not joost esplain to you
I weell no care w'at else you do
So long you don'ta sand to me
No peecture-card from Napoli?

The Caged Bird

Giacomo Sarpatti, lasta spreeng,
 Catcha seengin' bird upon a bush;
Freckles on da breast an' browna wing—
 How you call een Anglaice langwadge? "Thrush?"
Een Italia "tordo" ees da word;
Eet ees verra pretta seengin' bird.

Wal, he maka fina cage for eet,
 An' eet's een hees yard all summer long;
Early evra morn eet seenga sweet,
 Sweeta, too, da evenings weeth eets song.
"Ah!" he say, "so long my bird ees seeng,
Alla time for me eet ees da spreeng."

"W'en da weenter com'," say Giacomo,
 "Een my warma keetchen I no care;
I weell nevva mind da frost an' snow,
 For my bird weell maka summer dere.
Pretta soon I gona tak' heem een;
Jus' so soon da colda nights baygeen."

But he wait, dees Giacomo, too long!
 Out dere een da yard hees bird could see
Manny theengs dat mak' heem stop hees song;
 He could see all othra birds dat's free
Flyin' down da sky eento da Sout',
An' dere was no music een hees mout'.

Een da yard I see da cage today,
 But dere ees no bird een eet no more!
"W'at ees dees?" I ask heem, an' he say:
 "O! I jus' forgot to shut da door."
W'en I laugh, he growl an' tal me: "Hal!
I know justa how eet feel mysal'."

Da Queena Bee

Meester, eef you nevva see
Housa full weeth busy bee,
   Leetla workers an' deir queen,
I would like for takin' you
Where I eentroduce you to
   Giacobini's Pasqualin'.

She ees weedow, Pasqualin';
W'en dees fallow Giacobin'
Dies an' leaves her lasta fall,
He ain't leave mooch else at all;
Justa leetla baker-store
An' seex babies—notheeng more!
All are girls, dese babies, too;
W'at da deuce she gona do?
Wait, my frand, an' you weell know,
An' I bat you you could go
Manny mile bayfore you see
Soocha house for eendustry.
W'en her husband up an' die
She ain't got no time to cry;
She must work an' nevva stop.
Dere's da babies, dere's da shop,
An' da house dey're leevin' een;
She mus' keep dem fine an' clean—
An' da babies happy, too.
W'at da deuce she gona do?
Som' day I weell show to you;
Som' day you mus' go an' see
How dey play at "Busy Bee."
Com', su'pose eet ees da day
W'en at cleanin' house dey play:

28

Evra leetla girl weell stan'
Weeth her leetla brush een han',
Leetla bucket, leetla broom,
For to scrub an' sweep da room.
Den weell say dees Pasqualin':
"Leetla bees, I am your queen,
W'en I geeve da word baygeen;
Work an' seeng an' follow me,
Work an' seeng an' lat me see
Who can be da besta bee!"
Den dey laugh an' seeng an' go
Makin' joy weeth labor so
Eet ees done bayfore dey know.
So een all theengs, day by day,
Makin' work so lika play,
Pasqualina found da way!

Com', den, som' day we weell go,
An' you weell be proud to know
   Giacobini's Pasqualin';
An' dose leetla busy bee
W'en dey grow up, you weell see,
   Evra wan hersal' a queen!

Da Fightin' Irishman

Irishman he mak' me seeck!
He ees gat excit' so queeck,
    An' so queeck for fightin', too,
An', baysides, you nevva know
How you gona please heem. So
    W'ata deuce you gona do?

W'en I work een tranch wan day,
Irish boss he com' an' say:
"Evrawan een deesa tranch,
I no care eef he ees Franch,
Anglaice, Dago, Dootch or w'at,
Evrawan he musta gat
Leetla pieca green to show
For da San Patricio.
Dees ees Irish feasta day,
Go an' gat som' green!" he say,
"An' eef you no do eet, too,
I gon' poncha head on you!"
So I gat som' green to show
For da San Patricio.
Bimeby, 'nudder Irishman
He ees com' where I am stan',
An' he growl at me an' say:
"W'at you wearin' dat for, eh?
Mebbe so you theenk you be
Gooda Irishman like me.
Green ees jus' for Irishman,
No for dumb Eyetalian!
Tak' eet off!" he say, an', my!
He ees ponch me een da eye!

Irishman he mak' me seeck!
He ees gat excite' so queeck,
  Àn' so queeck for fightin', too,
An', baysides, you nevva know
How you gona please heem. So
  W'ata deuce you gona do?

Da Musica Man

You knowa Giovanni, da musica man?
He playa da harpa, he playa pian',
For maka da mona wherevra he can.
Da styleesha peopla dey geeve heem da chance
For maka da music for helpa dem dance.
   He playa da music so gooda, so gran',
He tal me, da ladies dey calla heem "sweet"
An' geeve heem da playnta good fooda for eat.
   I like be Giovanni, da musica man.

Giovanni, da musica man, he ees fat,
An' sleepy an' lazy so lika da cat,
So moocha da dreenkin' an' eatin' he gat.
I gotta da music eensida my heart;
I weesh I have also da musical art
   For mak' eet com' outa my heart like he can,
An' filla my stomach weeth fooda for eat.
I digga da tranch; I work hard on da street—
   I like be Giovanni, da musica man.

Een Court

I was een court wan day las' week,
　An' eet was strange to me.
I like eet not; steell, I would speak
　Of som'theeng dere I see.
To you, dat know da court so wal,
　I s'pose eet's notheeng new,
But you are kind, so lat me tal
　Dees leetla theeng to you:

Da "Judge"—I theenk dey call heem so—
　Da bossa for da place,
He's fine, beeg, han'som' man, an' O!
　Sooch kindness een da face.
Wal, soon dey breeng a pris'ner dere,
　A leetla boy; so small
Dat teell dey stand heem on a chair
　I did not see at all!
Poor leetla keed, I s'pose he might
　Be tan year old or less;
I nevva see sooch sorry sight,
　Sooch peecture of deestress.
"Dees ees a verra badda child,"
　Ees say da bigga cop
Dat hold hees arm; "he's runna wild,
　An' so I tak' heem up."
You theenk so smalla keed like dat
　Would cry, for be so scare';
But no, he tweest hees ragged hat
　An' justa nevva care.
Den speaks da Judge, an' O! so sweet,
　Like music ees hees voice.

He tals heem how da ceety street
  Ees notta place for boys.
At first da boy looks roun' da place,
  So like he nevva heard,
But soon he watch da Judge's face
  An' dreenks een evra word.
"My child, would you not like to go
  Where dere ees always food,
A gooda home, where you may grow
  For be da man you should?"
Da boy mak's swallers een hees throat
  As eef he try to speak,
But no wan near could hear a note,
  Hees voice eet was so weak.
"Eh? W'at was dat?" da Judge he said.
  "W'at deed you say, my dear?"
An' den he leaned hees han'som' head
  Down close to heem to hear.
I s'pose da boy's so strange, so wild,
  He deed not ondrastand;
He only knew dat Judge so mild
  Was sure to be hees frand.
An' so hees skeenny arms reached out—
  He deed not try to speak—
But, leeftin' up hees leetla mout'
  He keessed heem on da cheek!

O! hal, my frand, don't be ashame'
  For w'at ees een your eye!
Weeth me, weeth all, eet was da same,
  We could not help but cry;
Not tears for dat we was so sad,
  But for da joy to find
Wan leetla boy dat was so glad,
  Wan man dat was so kind!

34

Leetla Giuseppina

Joe Baratta's Giuseppina
  She's so cute as she can be;
Justa com' here from Messina,
  Weeth da resta family.
Joe had money in da banka—
  He been savin' for a year—
An' he breeng hees wife, Bianca,
  An' da three small children here.
First ees baby, Catarina,
    Nexta Paolo (w'at you call
    Een da Inglaice langwadge "Paul"),
    An' da smartest wan of all—
        Giuseppina!

Giuseppina justa seven,
  But so smart as she can be;
Wida-wake at night-time even,
  Dere's so mooch dat's strange to see.
W'at you theenk ees mos' surprise her?
  No; ees not da buildin's tall;
Eef, my frand, you would be wisa
  You mus' theenk of som'theeng small.
Eet's an ant! W'en first she seena
    Wan o' dem upon da ground,
    How she laughed an' danced around:
    "O! 'Formica,' he has found
        Giuseppina!"

"O!" she cried to heem, "Formica"
  (Dat's Italian name for heem),
"How you gatta here so queecka?
  For I know you no can sweem;

35

An' you was not on da sheepa,
  For I deed not see you dere.
How you evva mak' da treepa?
  Only birds can fly een air.
How you gat here from Messina?
    O! at las' I ondrastand!
    You have dugga through da land
    Jus' to find your leetla frand,
        Giuseppina!"

Da Wheestlin' Barber

Las' night you hear da op'ra?
  Eef you was uppa stair
An' eef you know Moralli
  You mebbe saw heem dere.
Moralli? He's a barber,
  But vera bright an' smart,
An' crazy for da op'ra;
  He knows dem all by heart.
He's alla tima wheestlin',
  An' often you can find
Jus' from da tune he wheestles
  W'at thoughts ees een hees mind.
Eef you would ask a question,
  Da answer you would gat
Ees notheeng but som' music—
  Ha! w'at you theenk of dat?

Las' week hees wife, Lucia—
  Fine woman, too, is she—
She gave to heem som' babies,
  Not only wan, but three!
Eef to your shop som' neighbors
  Should breeng sooch news to you
Eet sure would jus' excite you
  To say a word or two;
But deesa Joe Moralli,
  Dees music-crazy loon,
He never stopped hees wheestlin'—
  But justa changed hees tune.
Dees answer from hees music
  Was all dat dey could gat:

37

"Trio from 'Trovatore.'"
  Ha! w'at you theenk of dat?

He nevva stopped hees wheestlin'
  Dat "Trovatore" tune,
Not even w'en he's dreenkin'
  Weeth frands een da saloon.
He wheestled eet dat evenin'
  W'en home he went to see
Hees granda wife, Lucia,
  An' leetla babies three.
But w'en he stood bayfore dem
  He was so full weeth dreenk,
He looked upon dose babies
  An' wheestle—W'at you theenk?
O! den da tune he wheestled
  Was—how-you-call-eet?—"pat":
"Sextetta from Lucia."
  Ha! w'at you theenk of dat?

So Glad for Spreeng

Eef som'body com' today
To dees fruita-stan' an' say:
"W'at? Banana two for fi'?
Seems to me dat's verra high!"
I would look up een da sky
Where da sun ees shine so bright,
An' da clouds so sof' an' white
Sail like boats I use' to see
Een da bay at Napoli;
An' so softa theeng I am,
I would notta care a dam
Eef da customer should be
Sly enough for taka three!
Eef like dat you com' today
Mebbe so I justa say:

"See da Tony McAroni!
He ees verra lazy thing,
W'at da deuce he care for money?
Here ees com' da spreeng!"

Eef today I had a wife
An' she say: "My love! my life!
I mus' have fi'-dollar note
For da new spreeng hat an' coat,"
Theenk I gona grab her throat,
Bang her head agains' da wall?
Eh! Today? Oh, not at all!
She would look so pretta dere
Weeth da sunshine on her hair,
I would look at her, an' den
I would tal her: "Taka ten!"

Eef I had a wife today
I am sure dat I would say:
  "All right, Mrs. McAroni,
    I am verra softa theeng.
  W'at da deuce I care for money?
    Here ees com' da spreeng!"

Da Flute een Spreeng

Dere was a time w'en I could shoot
    Profess' Agrandinallo,
For dat he played upon da flute
All nighta long hees "toot! toot! toot!"
An' made a seeckness een my head
W'en I was layin' een my bed.
O! manny, manny time I swore
W'en he was livin' nexta door—
    Dat crazy music-fallow!

Wan day een March, wan happy day,
    Profess' Agrandinallo
He took hees theengs an' moved away
Where I no more could hear heem play.
Ah! den da nights was full with sleep,
So beautiful, so long an' deep!
An' I was glad dat nevva more
I gona hear heem nexta door—
    Dat crazy music-fallow!

But, ah! my frand, I deed not feel
    How mooch, how mooch I meesed heem,
How dear hees music was, onteell
Las' night beside my weendow-seell,
From som'where far off down da street,
I heard hees flute so soft an' sweet!
O! my, eet made my heart so glad
Dat was so lonely an' so sad
    I justa coulda keessed heem!

For Goodness' Sak'!

"For goodness' sak'!" She say to me—
Dees girl, dees Angela Mari'
Dat soon my wife ees gona be—
    "Bayfore I go for leeve weeth you,
      You gotta habit, you mus' br'ak;
   Dees swearin' talk eet weell not do,
      For goodness' sak'!"

"For goodness' sak'! eet's mak' me sad,"
She say, "for hear you speak so bad."
An' I say, "Wal, w'en I am mad,
    I feel eef I no swear a few
      Dat som'theeng sure ees gotta br'ak;
   So w'at da deuce I gona do,
      For goodness' sak'?"

" 'For goodness' sak'!' dat's joosta w'at
You oughta say w'en you are hot!"
She say; "So promise you weell not
    Mak' swear words now for seexa week,
      Or you can tak' your presents back!
   Here's strongest langwadge you must speak:
      'For goodness' sak'!' "

For goodness' sak' I'm tonga-tied,
So dat she weell be satisfied,
Dees girl dat gona be my bride;
    But you, you guys dat know me—Wal!
      I hope dat you weell not meestak'
   What I am theenkin' w'en I yal:
      "For goodness' sak'!"

Da Poleetica Boss

Giuseppe Baratta ees great politeesh';
   He w'at you call "Dago poleetica boss."
He peeck da best man for da Pres'dant poseesh',
   An' show how you vote jus' by maka da cross.
He say: "Nevva minda w'at som'body tal
   W'at dees man or dat man ees goin' do for you.
You no ondrastan' deesa theeng verra wal,
   So jus' wait an' see w'at I tal you to do."

Giuseppe he study an' theenk an' he work
   So hard for deescovra w'eech side eesa best,
Ees nobody else een da ceety Noo York
   So theen like he gat an' so needa da rest.
Ees holes een hees shoe where da toes ees steeck through;
   Hees clo'es dey are look jus' so bad as dey can.
He say: "Eet ees harda for know w'at to do—
   I guess we weell vote for da Democrat man."

But steell he work hard for be sure he ees right,
   An' study som' more; an' so—presto!—wan day,
He com' weetha face ees so shiny an' bright,
   I see dat at las' he ees find da right way.
He gotta new shoes an' new pants an' new coat
   An' looka so styleesh an' fine as he can.
He say: "Ees meestak'! We gon' chanja dat vote.
   Ees besta for vote for Republica man."

Giuseppe Baratta ees great politeesh';
   Hees heart ees so true an' hees brain ees so bright,
He work an' he study, baycause he no weesh
   For mak' up hees mind teell he sure he ees right.

43

Da Colda Feet

Da beggarman across da way
  Ees happy as can be;
He laugh an' weenk baycause he theenk
  He gotta joke on me.

O! my! O! my! how cold eet ees
  For stan' on deesa street!
Da weends blow like dey gona freeze
  Da shoes upon your feet.
I nevva see een deesa town
  So fierce da weentra storm;
I keepa hoppin' up an' down
  For mak' my feeta warm.
But beggarman across da way
  He stan' against da wall,
So like eet was a summer day;
  He ees no cold at all.
Ees justa box een fronta heem
  For hold hees teenna cup,
But he bayhava so eet seem
  A stove for warm heem up.
An' evra time he look an' see
  How colda man am I,
He justa weenk an' laugh at me
  So like he gona die!
An' so I leave dees fruita stan'
  An' walka 'cross da street
For see how ees dees beggarman
  Can keep so warma feet.
I look, an' dere I see da legs
  Dat prop heem by da wall

Ees notheeng more dan wooden pegs—
    He got no feet at all!

Eef colda feet should mak' you swear
    An' growl so bad as me,
I bat your life you would no care
    So mooch eef you could see
Da beggarman across da way,
    So happy as can be,
Dat laugh an' weenk baycause he theenk
    He gotta joke on me!

W'at's a "Noraysuicide"?

Irish Padre Tommeeckbride
Laugh so mooch an' hold hees side,
I no mak' heem ondrastan',
Dough I talk so good's I can,
W'en today I go for see
Eef he pleassa marry me.
Den he call me soocha name
Eet ees maka me ashame'.

"Pleassa, Padre"—so I speak—
"I want marry nexta week."
"So?" he look at me an' say,
"You be bapatiza, eh?"
"No," I say, "you are meestak';
Weddin's w'at I want you mak'."
Steell how mooch I am esplain
I no gat eet een hees brain.
Alla time he justa cries:
"Where an' w'en you bapatize?"
Den my Rosa's brothra Joe—
He ees weetha me, you know,
An' ees smart as he can be—
He ees wheespera to me.
"Oh!" I say, for now ees plain
Mebbe so w'at Padre mean,
"First we want da weddin' here;
Bapatisma nexta year!"
Den da Padre laugh an' say:
"Noraysuicida, eh?"

Why you laugha? Dat'sa shame,
Callin' poor man soocha name!
Why ees Padre Tommeeckbride
Call me "Noraysuicide"?

46

Da Thief

Eef poor man goes
An' stealsa rose
   Een Juna-time—
Wan leetla rose—
You gon' su'pose
   Dat dat'sa crime?

Eh! w'at? Den taka look at me,
For here bayfore your eyes you see
Wan thief dat ees so glad an' proud
He gona brag of eet out loud!
So moocha good I do, an' feel,
From dat wan leetla rose I steal,
Dat eef I gon' to jail today
Dey no could tak' my joy away.
So, lees'en! here ees how eet com':
Las' night w'en I am walkin' home
From work een hotta ceety street,
Ees sudden com' a smal so sweet
Eet maka heaven een my nose—
I look an' dere I see da rose!
Not wan, but manny, fine an' tall,
Dat peep at me above da wall.
So, too, I close my eyes an' find
Anudder peecture een my mind;
I see a house dat's small an' hot
Where manny pretta theengs ees not,
Where leetla woman, good an' true,
Ees work so hard da whole day through,
She's too wore out, w'en com's da night,
For smile an' mak' da housa bright.

47

But, presto! now I'm home an' she
Ees seettin' on da step weeth me.
Bambino, sleepin' on her breast,
Ees nevva know more sweeta rest,
An' nevva was sooch glad su'prise
Like now ees shina from her eyes;
An' all baycause tonight she wear
Wan leetla rose stuck een her hair.
She ees so please'! Eet mak' me feel
I shoulda sooner learned to steal!

Eef "thief's" my name
I feel no shame;
    Eet ees no crime—
Dat rose I got.
Eh! w'at? O! not
    Een Juna-time!

Da Greata Basaball

Oh! greata game ees basaball
   For yo'nga 'Merican.
But, O! my frand, ees not at all
   Da theeng for Dagoman.

O! lees'en, pleass', I tal to you
   About wan game we play
W'en grass ees green, an' sky ees blue
   An' eet ees holiday.
Spagatti say: "We taka treep
   For play da ball, an' see
Wheech side ees ween da champasheep
   For Leetla Eetaly."
So off for Polo Groun' we go
   Weeth basaball an' bat,
An' start da greata game, but, O!
   Eet ees no feenish yat!
Spolatro ees da boss for side
   Dat wait for catch da ball;
Spagatti nine ees first dat tried
   For knock eet over wall.
An' so Spagatti com' for bat.
   Aha! da greata man!
Da han's he got; so beeg, so fat,
   Ees like two bonch banan'.
Spolatro peetch da ball, an' dere
   Spagatti's bat ees sweeng,
An' queeck da ball up een da air
   Ees fly like annytheeng.
You know een deesa game ees man
   Dat's call da "lafta-fiel'."

Wal, dees wan keep peanutta-stan'
    An' like for seettin' steell.
An' dough dees ball Spagatti heet
    Ees passa by hees way,
He don'ta care a leetla beet
    Eef eet ees gon' all day.
Da "centra-fielda man"—you know
    Dat's nex' to heem—he call:
"Hi! why you don'ta jompa, Joe,
    An' run an' gat da ball?"
But Joe he justa seetta steell
    Teell ball ees outa sight.
Dees mak' so mad da centra-fiel'
    He ees baygeen to fight.
Den com'sa nudder man—you see,
    I don'ta know hees name,
Or how you call dees man, but he
    Ees beeg man een da game.
He ees da man dat mak' da rule
    For play da gama right,
An' so he go for dose two fool
    Out een da fiel' dat fight.
He push da centra-fielda 'way—
    An' soocha names he call!—
An' den he grabba Joe an' say:
    "Com', run an' gat da ball."
But Joe he growl an' tal heem: "No,
    Ees not for me at all.
Spagatti heet da ball, an' so
    Spagatti gat da ball!"

O! greata game ees basaball
    For yo'nga 'Merican.
But, O! my frand, ees not at all
    Da theeng for Dagoman.

The Temperamental Tommasso

Tommasso can have, eef he want,
"Arteestica temperamant,"
But me, I am gladda for steeck
To workin' weeth shovel an' peeck.

You nevva can tal
Verra wal
Jus' w'en eet ees gona bust out—
Dees theeng dat I'm talkin' about.
Dees fallow Tommasso Barratt'
He nevva have notheeng like dat
Een all da long tima w'en he
Ees deeg een da streeta weeth me.
But all for a sudden wan day
He throw down hees shovel an' say:
"I gona be music-arteest!
Too moocha good time I have meessed,
An' so I gon' start righta 'way.
I jus' can'ta help eet. I must,
Or som'theeng eenside me weell bust!"
An' so he ees study da art;
But now dat he's ready for start—
Tomorrow, you see, ees da day
He's gona baygeen for to play—
Eet don't mak' heem happy wan beet.
He no can be steell een hees seat,
But tweest alla 'round een hees chair
An' pull hees mustache an' hees hair.
I say to heem: "Don'ta be scare';
Keep coola!" He tal me: "I can't!
Arteestica temperamant
Eensida me mak' me excite'
For fear I no playa jus' right."

51

I bat he no sleep mooch tonight.
I no like hees shoes on *my* feet!
He mebbe weell faint on da street
Tomorrow, baycause he's excite'
An' sure won'ta do da theeng right.
You see, dees new musica-man
He don't verra wal ondrastan'
Da ways of da streeta-pian'.

Tommasso can have, eef he want,
"Arteestica temperamant,"
But me, I am gladda for steeck
To workin' weeth shovel an' peeck.

Da Faith of Aunta Rosa

You know my Aunta Rosa? No?
  I weesha dat you could;
She w'at you call "da leevin' saint,"
  Baycause she ees so good.
She got so greata, stronga faith,
  She don'ta nevva care
For doin' anytheeng at all
  But justa say her prayer.
She justa pray, an' pray, an' pray,
  An' work so hard at dat,
You theenk she would be gattin' theen
  Eenstead for gat so fat.
O! my, she gat so verra fat,
  Da doctor ees so scare',
He com' wan day to her an' say:
  "You mak' too moocha prayer;
Ees better do som' udder work
  An' tak' som' exercise."
My Aunta Rosa shak' her head
  An' justa leeft her eyes,
An' say: "I gotta faith so strong
  Dat I weell jus' baygeen
For pray dat I may lose da fat,
  An' soon I weell be theen."
So den she justa seet an' pray,
  So greata faith she feel,
An' nevva stop for anytheeng—
  Excep' for taka meal.
An' som' time, too, she seet an' mak'
  Da noise so loud an' deep;
Eet sounda verra mooch as eef
  She prayin' een her sleep.

So Aunta Rosa pray an' pray,
  But steell she gat more fat,
So fat she no can walk at all—
  Now, w'at you theenka dat?

Mus' be som' troubla een da sky;
  Mus' be ees som'theeng wrong!
Baycause eef Aunta Rosa got
  Da faith so great an' strong,
An' pray so hard dat eet ees all
  She gatta time to do,
I like som'body tal me why
  Her prayer ees no com' true!

W'en Spreeng Ees Com'

Oh! 'scusa, lady, 'scusa, pleass',
  For dat I stop an' stare;
I no can helpa do like dees
  W'en spreeng ees een da air.

I s'pose you know how moocha joy
Ees feell da heart of leetla boy,
W'en beeg parade ees passa by,
Eef he can climb da pole so high;
Or find on window-seell a seat
Where he can see da whola street,
An' watch da soldiers marcha 'way
An' hear da sweeta music play.
Ah! lady, eef dees joy you know,
You would no frown upon me so.
For, like da boy dat climb da pole,
From deep eensida me my soul—
My hongry, starva soul—ees rise
Onteell eet looka from my eyes
At all dat com' so sweet an' fair
W'en now da spreeng ees een da air;
At greena grass, at buddin' trees
Dat wave deir branches een da breeze,
At leetla birds dat hop an' seeng
Baycause dey are so glad for spreeng—
An' you dat look so pure, so sweet,
O! lady, *you* are part of eet!

So, 'scusa, lady, 'scusa, pleass',
  For dat I stop an' stare;
I no can helpa do like dees
  W'en spreeng ees een da air.

55

Tony Maratt'

Tony Maratt' eesa yo'ng 'Merican,
Born an' raise' up een dees beautiful lan'.
Padre from Genoa, madre from Rom',
Long tima seence to dees countra ees com'.
      Nevva mind dat!
Look at heem now! From da sola hees feet
      To da toppa hees hat,
Mos' evrawhere dat you walk een da street
Here ees mos' styleesh yo'ng man you can meet—
      Tony Maratt'.

Strong ees dees Tony Maratt', like hees Pa.
Ah! but hees heart eesa sof', like hees Ma.
So seence las' year, w'en hees padre ees die,
Tony Maratt' ain't do notheeng but cry.
      W'at you theenk dat?
"Padre ees worka too hard for hees pay,
      An' jus' see w'at he gat!
My! eet ees sad he should go deesa way;
Now I mus' leeve for da madre," ees say
      Tony Maratt'.

Madre Maratt', now da padre ees dead,
Gotta work harda for maka da bread.
Tony ees sad for da padre, but steell
Jus' for da madre he tryin' to feel
      Happy an' fat.
"Don'ta be scare', leetla madre," say he,
      "I no die lika dat.
I ain't gon' workin' at all, for, you see,
You ain't got nobody lefta but me—
      Tony Maratt'."

The Student

Speak not weeth Dagoman dat sweep da street;
  He ees too domb, Signor.
All sense he got ees een hees han's an' feet,
  Jus' dat an' notheeng more.
You laugh for hear heem talk an' mak' meestak',
  But, com', eef you would see
How smart som' Dago ees seet down an' mak'
  Som' leetla talk weeth me.
Com', let us talk of wisa theengs we know.
  So, now I weell baygeen:
Ees eet not strange, my frand, how aard-varks grow
  An' keep from gattin' theen?
Eet mus' be tough for eatin' ants an' sooch
  So like dese aard-varks do;
You bat my life, I would no like eet mooch,
  No more, I s'pose, would you—
W'at? "Aard-vark?" Sure! Eh, w'at ees dat you say?
  Som'theeng you nevva heard?
O, yes, "a-a-r-d-v-a-r-k";
  Dat's how ees spal da word.
Eet ees een book, da wisa book I read
  Dat tal all theengs you want.
Ees call' "da 'Mericana Cyclopaed";
  I buy me wan las' mont'.
An' lasta week I learn da firsta page;
  Nex' week I learna two.
You bat my life, w'en I am good old age
  I gon' know more dan you.
I am su'prise' how mooch you don'ta know;
  You are not smart, Signor.
Ah, wal, good-bye! Com' back een week or so,
  I learn you som'theeng more.

The Laggard in Love

Oh! Giuseppe da barber ees crazy weeth spreeng!
He's no good een da daytimes for doin' a theeng
But to theenk of da night an' da tunes he weell seeng.
Alla time w'en som' customer gat een hees chair,
He's so slow weeth da shave an' weeth cuttin' da hair,
Dat hees boss ain't do notheeng but grumble an' swear.
But Giuseppe no care
  For wan blessa blame theeng,
      But to play mandolina
      Where som' signorina
  Weell listen at night to da love-song he seeng.

Com' Giuseppe da barber last nighta too late
To da house of da Rosa an' stan' by da gate,
An' he seeng like Il Gatto dat cry for hees mate.
Soocha playnta love-music, sooch cooin', sooch sighs,
Soocha sounds from da heart—an' sooch looka su'prise
W'en he leeft hees face up an' stare eento my eyes
Lookin' down from da wall!
  Ah! Giuseppe, your call
      Should be starta more earla
      For catcha my girla,
  For w'en da spreeng's here *I* no workin' at all!

The Wedding Anniversary

Eef, mebbe so, you gotta wife
  Dat's good as mine to me,
You weell be glad for mak' her life
  So happy as can be.

Las' fall Carlotta tak' my han'
An' maka me wan happy man;
Wan year today she ees my mate,
An' so tonight we celebrate.
You theenk I would forgat da day
Dat poor sooch sunshine on my way?
Ah! no, I gona lat her see
How kinda husban' I can be;
How glad I am she ees so true,
How proud for all da work she do.
An' so for mak' her work for me
More easy dan eet use' to be,
An' show how mooch my heart ees stir'—
I buy a leetla geeft for her.

Carlotta got so pretta hair,
I buy her som'theeng nice for wear—
Eh? W'at? O! no, ees notta hat;
Ees som'theeng mooch more use dan dat.
Eet's leetla pad, so sof' an' theeck
An' stuff' weeth wool, dat she can steeck
On top da hair upon her head,
So lika leetla feathra bed.
Eet sure weell mak' her feela good
W'en she ees carry loada wood;
An' mebbe so eet help her, too,
For carry more dan now she do.

59

So mooch weeth love my heart ees stir'
I buy dees leetla geeft for her.

Eef, mebbe so, you gotta wife
   Dat's good as mine to me,
You, too, would try for mak' her life
   So happy as can be.

The Blossomy Barrow

Antonio Sarto ees buildin' a wall,
But maybe he nevva gon' feenish at all.
    Eet sure won'ta be
    Teell flower an' tree
An' all kinda growin' theengs sleep een da fall.

You see, deesa 'Tonio always ees want'
For leeve on a farm, so he buy wan las' mont'.
I s'posa som' day eet be verra nice place,
But shape dat he find eet een sure ees deesgrace;
Eet's busta so bad he must feexin' eet all,
An' firs' theeng he starta for build ees da wall.
Mysal' I go outa for see heem wan day,
An' dere I am catcha heem sweatin' away;
He's liftin' beeg stones from all parts of hees land
An' takin' dem up to da wall een hees hand!
I say to heem: "Tony, why don'ta you gat
Som' leetla wheel-barrow for help you weeth dat?"
"O! com' an' I show you w'at's matter," he said,
An' so we go look at hees tools een da shed.
Dere's fina beeg wheel-barrow dere on da floor,
But w'at do you s'pose? From een under da door
Som' mornin'-glor' vine have creep eento da shed,
An' beautiful flower, all purpla an' red,
Smile out from da vina so pretty an' green
Dat tweest round da wheel an' da sides da machine.
I look at dees Tony an' say to heem: "Wal?"
An' Tony he look back at me an' say: "Hal!
I no can bust up soocha beautiful theeng;
I work weeth my han's eef eet tak' teell nex' spreeng!"

61

Antonio Sarto ees buildin' a wall,
But maybe he nevva gon' feenish at all.
        Eet sure won'ta be
        Teell flower an' tree
An' all kinda growin' theengs sleep een da fall.

Trilogy of Padre Angelo

I. THE MATCHMAKING

Padre Angelo he say:
"Why you no gat married, eh?
You are maka playnta mon'
For gon' taka wife, my son."
"No; I am too beeza man
'Tandin' dees peanutta stan'.
I no gatta time for play
Fooleeshness weeth girls," I say.
"My! you don'ta tal me so?"
Ees say Padre Angelo.

Bimeby, mebbe two, t'ree day,
Younga girl she com' an' say:
"Padre Angelo ees here?
No? Eet eesa vera queer!
Heesa housakeepa say
I gon' find heem deesa way."
While she eesa speaka so
Ees com' Padre Angelo.
"Rosa! you are look for me?"
He ees say to her, an' she
Say: "Oh, pleass, go homa, queeck,
You are want' for som'wan seeck.
I am sand for find you here."
"Ah! da seecka-call, my dear.
Com'," say Padre Angelo,
"Deesa younga man ees Joe;
Shaka han's bayfore we go."
So I am shak' han's weeth her—
Leetla han' so sof' like fur—

63

Den she bow to me an' go
Weetha Padre Angelo.

Bimeby, s'pose two, t'ree day more
She ees com' jus' like bayfore,
An' she aska me: "You know
Where ees Padre Angelo?
Housakeep' she tal me wait
Eef he don't be vera late."
So I tal her taka seat
An' to hav' som' fruit for eat.
Den I talk to her an' she
Smila sweet an' talk to me;
How long time I donta know.
Den com' Padre Angelo.
"Oh," she say, "go homa queeck,
You are want' for som'wan seeck."
"My!" he say, "dese seecka-call!
I am gat no peace at·all."
"Oh, wal, com', my dear," he say,
An' he takin' her away.
I am sad for see her go
Weetha Padre Angelo.

Many times ees lika dat.
Peopla always seem for gat
Seecka when he ees away.
Rosa com' mos' evra day.
An' som' time she gotta stay
Pretta longa time, you know,
Teell com' Padre Angelo.
Steell I no gat any keeck
How mooch peopla gatta seeck;

64

I am feela glad dey do—
Rosa, she no keeckin', too.
Lasta night my Rosa she
Go to Padre weetha me,
An' I tal heem: "Pretta soon—
Mebbe so da firsta June—
Rosa gona be my wife!"
He ees s'prise', you bat my life!
"W'at?" he say, an' rub hees eyes,
"Dees ees soocha gladda s'prise!
My! you don'ta tal me so?"
Ees say Padre Angelo.

II. THE UNMAKING OF IT

Rosa Beppi she'sa got
Temper dat's so strong an' hot,
Ees no matter w'at you say,
W'en she's start for have her way
She's gon' have eet; you can bat
Evra cent you got on dat!
Theenk she gona mind her Pop?
She ain't even 'fraid of cop!
Even devil no could stop
Rosa Beppi w'en she gat
Foolish theengs eenside her hat.
Dat'sa why her Pop ees scare',
Dat'sa why he growl an' swear
W'en he see her walkin' out
Weeth Pasquale from da Sout'.

Eef, like Beppi, you are com'
From da countra nort' of Rome,

You would know dat man from Sout'
Ain'ta worth for talka 'bout.
Ees no wondra Beppi swear,
Growl an' grumbla lika bear.
W'en da Padre Angelo
Com' an' see heem actin' so,
He's su'prise' an' wanta know.
Beppi tal him. "Ah!" he say,
"I weell talk weeth her today,
So she stop dees walkin' out
Weeth Pasquale from da Sout'."

Beppi shak' hees head an' sigh.
He don't theenk eet's use for try,
But da Padre smile an' say:
"I weell speak weeth her today."
Pretta soon, bimeby, he do—
Only say wan word or two—
But so soon as he ees through
You should see da Rosa! My!
Dere's a fire from her eye,
Cutta through you lika knife.
She ees mad, you bat my life!
But no more she's walkin' out
Weeth Pasquale from da Sout'.

Beppi's gladdest man I know
W'en he see how theengsa go.
"My!" he say, "I am su'prise'
Church can be so strong an' wise."
"Yes," say Padre Angelo,
"Church ees always wisa so.
All I say to her ees dees:
'Rosa, I am moocha please'

66

Dat at las' you gotta beau.
He ain't verra good wan, no;
But you need no minda dat
Seence he's best dat you can gat.
So I'm glad for see you out
Weeth Pasquale from da Sout'.'"

III. THE VOCATION

Padre Angelo he say
Alla tima deesa way:
"Evratheeng weell be all right—
Leave eet to da Lord Almight'!"

Padre Angelo he's know
Rosa Galdi an' her beau—
Dat'sa Joe Gregorio—
Seence dey both was joost so high;
Rosa? Ha! you nevva meet
Yo'nga girl so good, so sweet!
Joe he's gooda boy, but queer—
First he's dere an' den he's here,
Mebbe so you know da kind—
Joosta can't mak' up hees mind. . . .
Wal, seence lasta fall, Signor,
Deesa Joe's een Baltimore;
Gotta gooda job, but tough,
An' he no can mak' enough
For be marri' like he want.
So, wan day dees lasta mont'
Soocha letter he ees write—
Eet'sa mak' her so excite'—
Right away she musta go
To da Padre Angelo. . . .

67

"Look!" she say, "he tal me now:
'I am gon' for be a pries',
Den my soul weell be at peace;
An', you are so gooda girl,
You, too, should forsak' da worl';
Go for be a nun—' Oh, my!"
Here poor Rosa start for cry;
Den da Padre Angelo
Pat her hand an' speaka so:
"Dees ees joost too bad, my dear,
But we must not eentrafere
Weeth da Lord's weell— But, for you
Convent life weell nevva do. . . .
Dere ees Joe's yo'ng couseen Jeem,
Why you no walk out weeth heem?"
"No!" she tal heem, "No! No! No!
I weell always lova Joe!"
"Wal," he say, "den you must do
Dees dat I am tal to you:
Write to Joe at once, today,
An' here's all dat you mus' say:
*'We are verra please' to hear
You gon' be a pries', my dear.
But I am so fond for fun
I could nevva be a nun;
Now w'en com's your couseen Jeem
Mebbe I go out weeth heem—
But be sure we gonna pray
Night an' mornin' dat you may
Mak' success een evra way.'*
Don'ta cry! Joost write heem dat
An' we'll see w'at we weell gat.
Evratheeng weell be all right—
Leave eet to da Lord Almight'."

68

Dat was only week ago—
But da Padre Angelo
Marry Rosa yestaday!
Pretta queeck, eh? W'at you say?
"Queeck for Couseen Jeem?" Oh, no,
Sure, of course, she marry Joe!
W'en he read da note she write
He's rush home da nexta night. . . .
Ha! da Padre he ees wise!
"No," he say, "I'm no su'prise';
Evratheeng turns out all right—
Leave eet to da Lord Almight'."

Carlotta's Indecision

I would lika mooch to know
Why Carlotta treat me so.
Evra time I ask eef she
Ees gon' marry weetha me,
First she smila, den she frown,
Den she look me up an' down,
Den she shak' her head an' say:
"I gon' tal you Chrees'mas Day."

Once w'en we are out for walk
An' I am begin to talk,
She say: "Don'ta speak no more.
O! com', scc dees jew'ler store.
My! jus' look dat di'mon' reeng!
Eet ees justa sweetes' theeng!
Only seexa-feefty, see?"
Dat's da way she teasa me,
Findin' theengs for talka 'bout
Jus' for mak' me shut my mout'.
Bimeby w'en she turn for go
I say: "Com', I musta know—"
"O!" she stamp her foot an' say:
"I gon' tal you Chrees'mas Day."

I would lika mooch to know
Why Carlotta treat me so.
W'ata for she always say:
"I gon' tal you Chrees'mas Day"?

Da Greata Stronga Man

You oughta see my Uncla Joe
  W'en he ees gatta mad.
He ees da strongest man I know
  W'en som'wan treat heem bad.
Hees eye eet flash like blazin' coal,
  An' w'en he ope hees mout'
He growla like you theenk hees soul
  Ees turna eenside out.
He eesa gat so stronga den
  An' swell so big an' fat,
Eet gona taka seexa men
  For justa hold hees hat!

You oughta see my Uncla Joe
  W'en he ees mad weeth you.
You bat my life! den you will know
  I eesa speaka true.
He gat so strong eenside of heem
  Eet mak' your hearta freeze,
An' eef he looka at som' cream
  Eet turna eento cheese.
Den you weell run, you bat my life!
  So fast as you can go,
An' throw away your gun or knife.
  Ha! strong man, Uncla Joe.

  .   .   .   .   .

You oughta see my Uncla Joe!
  Eet w'at you call "su'prise."
Las' night beeg Irish ponch heem so
  Eet close up bot' hees eyes.
O! my! he eesa looka bad;
  Mus' be ees som'theeng wrong,

71

Baycause w'en Uncla Joe ees mad
　　He always been so strong.
I guess dees Irish heet his blow
　　So queecka an' so rough
He no geeve time to Uncla Joe
　　For gatta mad enough.

Da Styleesha Lady

I tal you w'at, you oughta see
Carlotta, dat's my girl, w'en she
Ees feex' for holiday. I guess
You nevva see sooch styleeshness.
She gotta yallow seelka skirt
Ees look so fine you theenk ees wort'
'Bout twanty dollar, mebbe more,
Eef you gon' buy eet een da store.
So, too, she gotta purpla wais'
Dat's treem' weeth pretta yallow lace,
An' bigga golda breasta-peen
Ees steeckin' ondraneat' her cheen.
Eh? Wait, my frand! On toppa dat
She got da beega redda hat
Weeth coupla featha, brighta green,
An' whita rosa een baytween.
Da redda, whita, green, you see,
Ees lika flag of Italy!

Ha! w'at you theenka dat for style?
Ah! yes, my frand, eet mak' you smile;
You can eemagine, den, of me,
How proud I smile w'en first I see.
You can baylieve how proud I feel
For walkin' out weeth her; but steell
I gatta—w'at you call—"deestress"
Baycause for all dees styleeshness.
You see, w'en she ees look so sweet
I 'fraid for let her on da street.
I justa feela scare' dat som'
Beeg reecha man ees gona com'
An' see how styleesh she can be,
An' steala her away from me.

73

Mr. Hail Colomb'

Irish, Anglaice, Dootchman, Jew,
W'at'sa matter weetha you?
Why you no keep holiday,
Wave da flag an' shout "Hooray"?
Why you laugh an' weenk your eye
W'en da beeg parade go by?
Ain't you glad for anytheeng
W'en da leetla cheeldren seeng?
Lika me you oughta be
Glad for granda liberty
Dat you all are gattin' from
      Hail Colomb'.

Can eet be you are so domb
You don't know dees "Hail Colomb'"?
He ees Dago sailorman
Firsta find dees greata lan'.
Poor he was, but, O! rejoice,
Tak' your hat off, leeft your voice,
Maka prayer of thanks baycause
Dere's no Eemigration laws,
Dere's no Ellis Island w'en
Weeth hees ragged sailormen
First to deesa shores ees com'
      Hail Colomb'.

A Lesson in Politics

I no care for gattin' meex'
Een dees ceety politeecs.
I no gatta vote, an' so
I no weeshin' mooch to know
W'eech side right an' w'eech side wrong:
I no bother mooch so long
Dey no bother mooch weeth me—
I jus' want do beez'ness, see?

I no like poleecaman
Com' to dees peanutta-stan',
Like he do most evra day,
Jus' for talka deesa way:
"Wal, my frand, I tal you w'at,
Politeecs ees gattin' hot.
Don't you mind all deesa queer
Talka 'bout da 'Graft' you hear.
Notheeng een eet!" (Here he tak'
Bigga pieca geenger cak'.)
"Dees 'Reforma' mak' me seeck!
Sucha foolish theengs dey speak!
All dees 'graft' ees een deir eye."
(Now he taka pieca pie.)
"I been een dees politeecs
Seexa year an' know da treecks,
But I tal you I ain't met
Any kinda grafta yet."
(Here he taka two banan'.)
"Evra publeec office man
Worka for a salary
Jus' da sama lika me.

We no want no more dan dat—
Jus' contant weeth w'at we gat."
(Den he tak' weeth botha hand
Som' peanutta.) "So, my frand,
Don't baylieve all deesa queer
Talka 'bouta 'graft' you hear."

Nutta, caka, pie, banan',
All for wan poleecaman!
Mebbe ees no "grafta"—say!
W'at ees "grafta," anyway?

Da Younga 'Merican

I mysal', I feela strange
   Een dees countra. I can no
Mak' mysal' agen an' change
   Eento 'Merican, an' so
I am w'at you calla me,
   Justa "dumb ole Dagoman."
Alla same my boy ees be
   Smarta younga 'Merican.
Twalv' year ole! but alla same
   He ees learna soocha lot
He can read an' write hees name—
   Smarta keed? I tal you w'at!

He no talk Italian;
   He say: "Dat's for Dagoes speak,
I am younga 'Merican,
   Dago langwadge mak' me seeck."
Eef you gona tal heem, too,
   He ees "leetla Dago," my!
He ees gat so mad weeth you
   He gon' ponch you een da eye.
Mebbe so you gona mak'
   Fool weeth heem—an' mebbe not.
Queeck as flash he sass you back;
   Smarta keed? I tal you w'at!

He ees moocha 'shame' for be
   Meexa weeth Italian;
He ees moocha 'shame' of me—
   I am dumb ole Dagoman.
Evra time w'en I go out
   Weetha heem I no can speak

To som'body. "Shut your mout',"
    He weell tal me pretta queeck,
"You weell geeve yoursal' away
    Talkin' Dago lika dat;
Try be 'Merican," he say—
    Smarta keed? I tal you w'at!

I am w'at you calla me,
    Justa "dumb ole Dagoman";
Alla same my boy ees be
    Smarta younga 'Merican.

Da Styleesha Wife

Giuseppe, da barber, ees catcha da wife!
O! my, you weell laugh w'en you see w'at he gat.
She gotta da face ees so sharp like da knife—
He say: "Ees no styleesh for face to be fat."
Her fingers, so skeenny, ees notheeng but bone;
You 'fraid dey weell bust w'en you go for shak' han'.
He say: "Dat'sa sign she ees vera high-tone',
She no gotta han's like two bonch da banan'."
             Ha! w'at you theenk dat
             For talk een hees hat?
W'at good eesa wife eef she don'ta be fat?

Giuseppe, he tal me I no ondrastan'
Da 'Merican lady so gooda like heem;
He tal me hees wife ees da "swell 'Merican,"
An' looka so styleesh baycause she ees "sleem."
I tal heem da "styleeshness" notta so good
For keepa da house an' for helpin' her mooch
To nursa da baby an' carry da wood.
He say: "I no care eef she nevva do sooch."
             Ha! w'at you theenk dat
             For talk een hees hat?
W'at good eesa wife eef she don'ta be fat?

Beezaness? Fine!

Who say dat beezaness ees blue
An' times ees hard? Eet ees not true.
   You bat my life! I nevva see
   Sooch trade like now ees com' to me.
Ah! lees'en, an' I tal to you.

Last fall w'en first I com', my frand,
For keep dees small peanutta stand,
Eet was too playnta beeg enough,
Baycause I sal so leetla stuff,
But now so manny com' for buy
Banan', an' peach, an' cak' an' pie,
I soon must gat, I am afraid,
Fine bigga store for serve my trade.
Den, mebbe, too, I gonna see
To sal da coffee, milk an' tea
For customer dat aska me.

You be su'prise' for see how fine
Ees all dese customer of mine;
An' so polite dey eat deir food,
An' look so reech, an' talk so good—
An' mosta talk dey mak' ees "How
Da stocka mark' ees actin' now?"
Oh, dere ees wan, so beeg, so tall,
He ees da grandest wan of all!
An' w'en he eat hees pie, my frand,
An' I am watch heem go an' stand
Een doorway of dat beeg hotal
On Broada Street, dat ees so swal,
An' see heem peeck hees teeth, an' smile
An' bow een soocha granda style

To all hees frands dat passa by,
I am so proud I like to die!

Eef times ees hard you s'pose I gat
So fina, bigga trade like dat?
From all dat I am tal to you
Can dees "bad beezness" talk be true?
  Eh, w'at?
  I bat you, not!

Da Horsa-Race

Joe Cavalieri, he's w'at-you-call "jay!"
So dumb, he do evratheeng jus' da wrong way.
  You nevva can turn 'eem
   Da right way, or learn 'eem—
He jus' maka face to whatevra you say.

For eenstance, een weenter he walks on da street
Weeth socks on da outside da shoes on hees feet!
An' always on toppa hees head you weell see
Da back of hees cap where da front oughta be.
He's gotta wan beeg, bony horse he call "Jack"—
You see, deesa Joe eesa diggin'-contrac'—
An' dough he don't quite put da horse een da back
An' da cart een da front, eet ees true, for a fac',
He's learna dees horse eet's a sign he shall go
More fast an' more fast w'en he call to heem: "Whoa!"
Ha! w'at you theenk dat for dees cocket-eye Joe?
But Joe he don't care; eet no bother heem none
W'en othra contrac's ees start pokin' da fun,
But wan o' dose guys makin' cracks dat'sa wise
Ees Tony Baratta—an' he gats su'prise!
Joe looks at heem cold, an' he says to heem: "Tony,
You theenka my horse ees so slow an' so bony,
Eef mebbe you got hundred dollar—good money—
You bat on your horse an' I bat on my Jack
An' we drive dem right now on da horsa-race track!"

So Tony an' Joe, weeth da cart an' da horse,
Dey race for da—how-you-call?—"Two Hunder Purse,"
An' all of our people ees out eena force.
A guy weetha peestol goes "Bang!" an' dey start!
"Hooray!" shout da people; bump! bump! goes da cart.

82

Eet looks as eef Joe eesa poosh on da reins,
But steell for all dat eet ees Tony dat gains,
Hees horse ees so strong an' ees jompin' so fine
He looks to be sure da first over da line—
But, joost w'en dey com' een da stretch, deesa Joe
He steeck out hees cheen an' he holler: "Whoa! Whoa!"
Oh, my, you should see dat old bony horse go!
Of course, dat was joost da right word for hees Jack,
But Tony's horse heard an' stopped dead een hees track!
An' long bayfore Tony can mak' heem go on
Dees Joe an' hees Jack dey have winna da mon'—
Ha! w'at you theenk dat for a sunovagun?

Joe Cavalieri, he's w'at-you-call "jay";
So dumb, he do evratheeng joost da wrong way.
    You nevva can turn 'eem
    Da right way, or learn 'eem
He jus' maka face to w'atevra you say!

Een Napoli

Here een Noo Yorka, where am I
Seence I am landa las' July,
All gray an' ogly ees da sky,
    An' cold as eet can be.
But steell so long I maka mon',
So long ees worka to be done,
I can forgat how shines da sun
    Een Napoli.

But oh, w'en pass da boy dat sal
Da violets, an' I can smal
How sweet dey are, I no can tal
    How seeck my heart ees be.
I no can work, how mooch I try,
But only seet an' wondra why
I could not justa leeve an' die
    Een Napoli.

The Lonely Honeymoon

You know dees Joe dat use' to go
  For work weeth me, Signor?
He's marry, yestaday, you know,
  An' gon' for Baltimore;
An' so deesgusta man like Joe
  You nevva see bayfore!

Eh? No, da girl's all right, my frand;
  Dat's mak' eet harder, too.
Ha! wait an' you weell ondrastand—
  I tal eet all to you.
You see, dees Joe long time ago
  Gat Rosa for hees mash,
An' evra seence he worka so
  For mak' an' save da cash,
Baycause he want gat marry soon
  An' mebbe takin', too,
Dees—w'at you calla—"honeymoon,"
  Like 'Mericana do.
Wan day he tak' fi'-dollar note
  An' go to steamsheep store
An' buy two teecket for da boat
  Dat sail for Baltimore.
An' den he tal me: "Shut your mout'
  An' justa looka wise.
Dees theeng ees no for talka 'bout;
  Eet gona be su'prise."
So, w'en dey marry yestaday
  He smile so proud, Signor,
W'en he ees keess her cheek an' say:
  "We sail for Baltimore!"

85

Ah! den, my frand, so sadda sight
　　You nevva see. Oh, my!
Poor Rosa she ees gat so white
　　An' ees baygeen to cry.
"Ees dees," she say, "a weddin' treep?
　　Sooch fooleeshness you speak!
I no can stand eet een a sheep,
　　Da sea ees mak' me seeck."
Poor Joe, he swear an' den he keess,
　　An' coax an' beg her so,
For theenk of all dat she weell meess—
　　But no, she weell no go.
"O! Rosa mia!" Joe ees cry,
　　"Your heart eet ees a stone,
For dat you mak' me say 'good-bye'
　　An' tak' da treep alone!"

Oh, lonely honeymoon, an' oh,
　　So sadda man, Signor,
Dat gotta leave hees wife an' go
　　Alone for Baltimore!
So hearta-broka man like Joe
　　You nevva see bayfore.

Apologia pro Vita Sua

W'at for you call me "Dagoman,"
   An' mak' so bada face?
Ees no room for Eetalian
   Een deesa bigga place?

I s'pose you are more better dan
   Da Dagoman could be.
But, pleassa, Meester 'Merican,
   I ask you wait and see.
How long you leeve een deesa land?
   Eh? Thirta-seven year?
Ees onla seexa mont', my frand,
   Seence I am comin' here.
I weesh you geeve me time for try
   An' see w'at I can do,
So mebbe I gon' be, bimeby,
   So gooda man like you.
Baycause I am so strong, I guess
   I gon' do pretta wal.
So long I 'tand to beezaness
   An' jus' bayhave mysal'.
My leetla cheeldren, too, ees strong—
   Eh? You no gotta none?
You married, Meester? Eh? How long?
   Twalve year! an' no got wan?
Oh, I am sad for you, my frand—
   Eh? Why you laugh at me?
Escuse! I do not ondrastand;
   I am so strange, you see.
My "keeds ees no good breed," you say?
   Ah! wal, ees mebbe not,

But dey weell be more good som' day
  Dan dose you don'ta got;
An' dey be stronga 'Merican,
  More strong dan you are, too.
Ees notta many Dagoman
  So skeenny lika you.
Oh! pleass, my frand, no gatta mad!
  Shak' han' bayfore you go.
Escusa me! I am so sad
  For speakin' to you so.

But why you call me "Dagoman"
  An' mak' so bada face?
Ees no room for Eetalian
  Een deesa bigga place?

The Love-song

You often hear me speak of Joe,
Da barber—Joe Baruccio?
An' Giacomo Soldini? He
Ees fruita merchant lika me.
   Wal, dey are love da sama signorina.
Dees fallow from da barber shop
He use' for seeng weeth Granda Op',
An' Giacomo, he ees so slow
He was no good at all w'en Joe
   Would seeng to her an' play da mandolina.

"Maria mia! days are long"
(So made dees fallow Joe hees song),
"Baycause dey keepa me so far
From where you are, O! brighta star,
      Maria mia!"
An' Giacomo, w'at could he do?
He jus' would say w'en Joe was through:
      "Me, too, Maria!"

Dees Joe he deed not care at all,
W'en he would go to mak' hees call,
Eef Giacomo was also near;
He was so proud he deed not fear
   Dat annywan could steal dat signorina.
Deed he not have da sweeta voice
For mak' da female heart rejoice?
But ah! Maria, deed she care
Dat annybody else was dere
   To hear heem seeng an' play da mandolina?

"Maria mia! eet ees wrong"
(So made dees Joe wan night hees song)
"To waste your time weeth two or three
W'en you could be alone weeth me,
        Maria mia!"
Poor Giacomo! w'at could he do?
He jus' could say w'en Joe was through:
        "Me, too, Maria!"

Maria laugh an' shak' her head;
Her eye ees bright, her cheek ees red.
An' when she rise up from her chair
An' stan' bayfore dose lovers dere,
    You nevva see so pretta signorina.
"We wasta time," she say, "too long;
So now I, too, weell seeng a song;
An' deesa song dat I weell seeng
Eet ees so verra leetla theeng
    I weell not need at all da mandolina:

    " 'Maria mia!' so you seeng,
    But lova-song ain't everatheeng!
So, Joe, good-night! But you—O! stay,
My Giacomo, dat jus' can say:
        'Me, too, Maria!' "
Ah! Giacomo, w'at could he do?
He jus' could say, w'en she was through:
        "Me? O! Maria!"

Da Blue Devil

Som'time w'en I no feela good
  An' beezaness ees flat,
I gat so blue I weesh I could
  Be justa dog or cat.
W'en evratheeng ees gona wrong
  An' I mus' feex eet right,
I gat deesgust' for work so long
  An' theenk would be delight
For be a leetla cat, baycause
  Da only work she do
Ees wash her face an' leeck her paws,
  An' after dat she through.
Eef you be dog you jus' can go
  For sleepin' een da sun,
An' you don't got a wife, you know,
  For aska you for mon'.
Eet's mak' no odds how you behave
  Eef you are animal;
You don't got any soul to save,
  An' when you die, dat's all!
O! my, how easy kind of life
  For justa nevva mind,
To run away an' leave your wife
  An' evratheeng bayhind!

Dees ees da way I feela w'en
  I'm blue, but, alla same,
W'en I am feel all right agen
  Eet mak'sa me ashame'.
W'en devil gat eenside o' me
  For mak' me feel like dat,
I guess I would not even be
  A decen' dog or cat.

HIBERNICE

Spring in the Blood

If, when spring is in the blood,
  ('Tis of Irish blood I'm speakin')
All the peace o' bachelorhood
  Glad ye'd be to be forsakin'
    For the hope o' joy that lies
    In a pair o' sparklin' eyes
      Wishful to possess ye,
    Take your chance o' paradise
      An' Heaven bless ye!

If, when spring is in the blood,
  Grosser appetites awaken,
An' ye feel a thirst that could,
  Maybe, bear a little slakin'—
    If to clear your throat o' dust
    Mountain-dew will ease ye, just—
      Sure, I'd never chide ye.
    Take your tipple if ye must,
      An' Wisdom guide ye!

If, when spring is in the blood,
  Weary on your toil, ye're wishin'
You could wander through the wood
  Where the other lads are fishin';
    If such sport as ye could know
    Where the Irish rivers flow
      Waters here can lend ye,
    Seize your day of pleasure; go,
      An' Luck attend ye!

If, when spring is in the blood,
  Play-boy pranks nor eyes o' woman

Stir your heart-strings as they should,
  Faith, ye're somethin' less than human!
    What ye need's another birth;
    Though, indeed, 'twould not be worth
     All the trouble to remake ye.
    Fit for neither heaven nor earth,
     The Divil take ye!

The Irish Bachelor

Here fur yer pity or scorn, I'm presintin' ye
       Jerry McGlone.
Trustin' the life of him will be previntin' ye
       Marrin' yer own.
Think of a face wid a permanint fixture of
Looks that are always suggistin' a mixture of
Limmons an' vinegar. There! ye've a pixture of
       Jerry McGlone.

Faix, there is nothin' but sourest gloom in this
       Jerry McGlone.
Chris'mas joy, anny joy, never finds room in this
       Crayture of stone.
Cynical gloom is the boast an' the pride of him,
An' if a laugh ever did pierce the hide of him,
Faix, I believe 'twould immajiate, inside of him,
       Change to a groan.

Whisht! now, an' listen. I'll tell ye the throuble wid
       Jerry McGlone.
He preferred single life rather than double wid
       Molly Malone.
Think of it! Think of an Irishman tarryin'
While there's a purty girl wishful fur marryin'!
Arrah! no wonder the divils are harryin'
       Jerry McGlone.

Ah! but there's few o' the race but would scorn to be
       Jerry McGlone.
Sure, we all know that a Celt is not born to be
       Livin' alone.

Oh, but we're grateful (I speak for the laity)
Grateful fur women the bountiful Deity
Dowers wid beauty an' virtue an' gaiety,
    All for our own!

Kitty's Graduation

Dublin Alley jisht was crazy, jubilation was the rule,
Chewsday week whin Kitty Casey won the honors at the school.
Sure, the neighbors had been waitin', all impatient of delay,
For to see her graduatin' on that most important day.
Eddication is a power, an' we owned wid one accord
Casey's girl's the sweetest flower ever blossomed in the ward,
Whin, wid dress white as the daisy, but wid cheeks that shamed
   the rose,
We beheld wee Kitty Casey in her graduation clo'es.

Now, this Casey loved his daughther in a most indulgent way,
An' he spent his gold like wather for her graduation day.
Sich a dale of great preparin'! Sure, ye'd think she was a bride;
Sorra hair was Casey carin' for a blessed thing beside.
For whin Casey once comminces, faith, he never stops at all,
An' he dressed her like a princess at a Coronation Ball.
An' 'twas Madame Brigette Tracy for dressmaker that he chose,
For to fit out Kitty Casey in her graduation clo'es.

Of dressmakers, now, the oddest was this one that Casey'd got,
For her bill-heads called her "Modiste," though the prices there
   did not.
"But," sez Casey, "I can stan' it for to pay a few more cints,
So jisht go ahead an' plan it, ma'am, raygardless of ixpinse."
"Bong Moonseer," sez she, "I'll try it if she have the 'savoir fair.' "
"As fur that," sez Casey, "buy it, wid the other things she'll
   wear."
So ye see the man was crazy for to get the best that goes
For his little Kitty Casey in her graduation clo'es.

All the women jisht were itchin' for to see her gettin' dressed,
Some were crowded in the kitchen an' the stairway, while the
   rest,

The most favored ones, wint rushin' to the livin' room above,
Where stood Mrs. Casey blushin' wid a mother's pride an' love.
"Oh!" sez she, " 'twould be a pity if I couldn't schame an' plan
So that Kitty'd look as pritty as Mag Ryan's Mary Ann."
"Tut! ye needn't be onaisy," sez a neighbor. "Goodness knows,
There'll be none like Kitty Casey in her graduation clo'es."

An' there's really no denyin', whin they marched into the hall
Kitty Casey pushed the Ryan girl complately to the wall.
Whin she made her prize oration an' they gave her her degree,
There was sich a dimonstration as ye'll never live to see.
For the men from Dublin Alley voiced their feelin's in a cheer
Like they utther whin they rally in a Dimmycratic year,
An' of Casey's proudest days he counts that best of all he knows
Which beheld his Kitty Casey in her graduation clo'es.

Father O'Shea and Father McCrea

Ye might search the world's ends,
But ye'd find no such friends
  As Father O'Shea an' Father McCrea.
      Very caustic in wit
        Was Father O'Shea,
      But as droll every bit
        Was Father McCrea;
An' O! such a volley o' fun they were pokin',
  The wan at the other, as good as a play,
Wid their ready replies an' their innocint jokin',
  When Father O'Shea met Father McCrea.

Now, upon a March Sunday it came for to pass
      Good Father McCrea
Preached a very fine sermon an' then, afther Mass,
      Met Father O'Shea.
" 'Twas a very appropriate sermon for Lent
  Ye delivered this minute.
For the season o' fastin' 'twas very well meant—
  I could find no meat in it!"
      Said Father O'Shea.

Then, quick as the laughther that gleamed in his eye,
      Good Father McCrea
Raised a finger o' protest an' made his reply
      To Father O'Shea.
"Faith, I'll have to be workin' a miracle next,
  To comply wid your wishes.
Dare you ask me for meat, my dear sir, when the text
  Was 'the loaves an' the fishes'?"
      Said Father McCrea.

Very caustic in wit
        Was Father O'Shea,
But as droll every bit
        Was Father McCrea;
Though ye'd search the world's ends
Ye would find no such friends
        As Father O'Shea an' Father McCrea.

The Omadhaun

The lads that wastes their days in school,
 They nod an' wink an' call me "fool,"
But, och! 'tis little mind I have to scold them.
 Wid all their books they've never read
 The half of all that's in me head;
They couldn't un'erstan' it if I told them.

Did y' ever catch a leprechawn?
Ye never did! For why? 'Tis gone
Before ye know the crayture's nigh;
For if ye held him wid yer eye
He'd have to take ye to the spot
Where all his gold is in the pot.
But me they never hold in fear—
Small care have fools for gold an' gear—
So when they meet me on me way
They stop to pass the time o' day.
Did y' ever know the funny things
A thrush can tell ye? When he sings
Close both yer ears wid ayther han'
An' then as quick as e'er ye can
L'ave loose, hold tight, l'ave loose, hold tight—
But, och! ye'd never do it right!
Did y' ever know just how and when
'Tis aisiest to catch a wren?
"The wren, the wren, the king o' birds,
St. Stephen's Day, caught in the furze!"
Lasht Stephen's Day mayhap ye heard
Who was it snared the nimble bird
Upon the bush that through the town
The lads paraded up and down,

The while they begged from door to door,
The jinglin' coppers by the score.
'Twas me! I snared the wren an' got
No ha'penny of all the lot.
Not wan for me! They were so mean
They spint it all at Kane's shebeen.

Och, l'ave them wink an' call me "fool,"
Them lads that wastes their days in school,
An' oulder wans that spiles their brains wid drinkin'.
'Tis they're the fools themsel's, no less,
For sorra wan o' them could guess
The knowledgable things I do be thinkin'.

The Two Blind Men

Good avenin' to ye, Father; will ye be to bide a minyit?
  'Tis a week o' weeks since ye was here before.
There' manny feet goes up the sthreet, an' once yer own was in
    it—
  Last night I heard your footsteps pass me door.
Och! musha, Father, who am I to stop a priest that's passin' by
  To wan that needs him more?

Aye! "Conor o' the Brooms." I know; he bragged of it this
    mornin',
  Wid a dale o' windy wurrds, "sez I," "sez he."
Ye may go bail he'd make the tale, wid fanciful adornin',
  As wonderful as anny tale could be.
Sure, Father, 'tis mesel' that's glad ye wint to cheer yon poor
    ould lad,
  That's blinder far nor me.

O, yes, there *is* a differ, though, I'm free to be admittin',
  Ways, the two of us is blind as anny stone.
But times, ye see, Con sez to me: "I feel so blind jist sittin'
  Wid no wan nigh, jist sittin' by me lone."
They're blind indeed, poor souls, that need another's mind to see
    and read
  What thoughts are in their own.

So ye needn't think I'm jealous of a lad like poor ould Conor,
  Fur me own mind's stored wid company galore;
An' 'tis little I'll be carin'—though I thank ye fur the honor—
  If ye're passin' by or stoppin' at me door.
Sure, ye're welcome, Father Mack, but I'd never call ye back
  From wan that needs ye more.

The Son of His Father

Oh! my, oh! my, the years go by
  Like sheep the dogs are harryin';
But late I had a lispin' lad,
  An' now he talks o' marryin'!
Lord bless me! but he has the strut
  Of one that's grand an' knows it;
No lass so prim that looks at him
  But likes his cut an' shows it.
An', oh, 'twould do your heart good, too,
  To hear him at the blarney;
There's scarce a lass that sees him pass
  But wears a smile for Barney—
      Ōur Barney—
    A wishful smile for Barney.

Tho' Cupid lays cute snares these days
  When Barney goes philanderin',
An' all his traps hold geese, perhaps,
  None takes this bold young gander in.
Ah! none as yet, but there's a net
  That will, one day or other,
An' her I'd name to bait the same
  Is one like me, his mother.
Aye! sure as fate, he'll take for mate
  Sweet, roguish Nora Kearney,
Who meets his wiles with scornful smiles,
  As once I did with Barney—
      My Barney,
    The father of "our" Barney.

The Homing Girl

'Twas the gran' time the girls had at Katie Breen's th'-day
    To sind off wid God-speed her cousin, Mary Carr,
Fur 'tis Mary is the wise girl that laid away her pay,
    An' now she's fur the ould home away in Castlebar.
'Twas Kate Breen, the good soul, that got the party up
    An' passed 'round the kind word for ev'rywan to come,
Fur th' ould fr'inds to drop in an' have the bit an' sup,
    An' cheer the heart o' Mary Carr before she started home.
'Twas mesel' came whin Mary came this manny year ago,
    So gladly an' proudly I wint th'-day to call,
An' I walked in me fine clo'es wid Patrick Kane, me beau;
    But now I am the sorry girl I ever wint at all.

Sure, Mary Carr's the plain thing, an' timid as a mouse—
    'Tis small wonder no man had ever liked her style—
But the sorra wan of all thim that gathered in the house
    Had the half o' the happiness that twinkled in her smile,
Whin she spoke o' the ould joys she'd dreamed so much about—
    The green grass, the glad birds, the blessid Irish sky.
Then wan girl, a young girl that hadn't long been out,
    She flung up her two han's an' oh, but she did cry.
The girls looked at Mary Carr an' all their eyes were dim,
    An' I looked at Patrick Kane a-standin' be the wall,
There was pride, aye! an' comfort in the thought o' havin' him,
    But, oh, I was the sorry girl I'd ever come at all.

An' walkin' home, the two of us, he axed me why I cried.
    "Sure," sez I, "who wouldn't cry fur sake o' Mary Carr?"
Oh, it was the black lie, an' sure, I knew I lied—
    Not a wan of all me tears but fell for Castlebar!
'Twas Mary Carr that came wid me this manny year ago,
    Now 'tis she that's turnin' back an' bound fur home alone.

107

Still, should I be grudgin' her the ould delights she'll know?
  Haven't I a newer joy an' sweeter fur me own?
Oh, Patrick Kane's the good man an' fond as wan could be;
  An' sure I was the proud girl that walked wid him to call
On Mary Carr that's not the half as fortunit as me—
  But, oh, I am the sorry girl I ever wint at all.

Mona Machree

Mona Machree, I'm the wanderin' creature now,
            Over the sea;
Slave of no lass, but a lover of Nature, now,
            Careless an' free.
Nature, the goddess of myriad graces,
Pours for lorn lovers a balm that effaces
Scars from the heart, in these smilin' new places
  Far to the eastward an' far to the south of you.
Sweet are the grapes that she gives me to eat,
Red are her pomegranates, luscious an' sweet,
Dreamy the breath of her flowers in the heat—
  But, oh, the red mouth of you,
            Mona Machree!

Mona Machree, though it's here that the money is,
            Rather for me
Dreams an' drowsed rovin's through blooms where the honey is,
            Wild as a bee.
She, the new goddess to whom I'm beholden,
Snares me in days that are scented an' golden
E'en as the tresses your temples enfoldin',
  Aye, an' the blue, when the sun has forsaken it,
Blossoms with jewels, night-lamps of her throne,
Bright as two passionless eyes I have known.
Ah! it is here that my heart is my own—
  But, oh, the dull ache in it,
            Mona Machree!

The Golden Girl

Red hair!
Isn't it quare?
Once on a time I'd do nothin' but jeer at it.
Now, faith,
Look at me teeth,
See how I show them an' growl when you sneer at it.

Brown eyes?
"Muddy wid lies,"
"Dull an' deceitful," I once was decidin' them;
But—whack!—
Yours will go black
Under me fist now, if you'd be deridin' them.

What's more,
Freckles galore
Made a complexion the worst I could deem of it;
But now—
You must allow
They give a touch o' pure gold to the cream of it.

Some girls
Flaunt the red curls,
But it is blue eyes inundher that gaze at ye;
Some own
Freckles alone—
Let them be oglin' as much as they pl'ase at ye.

One charm
Needn't alarm;
Fear not the lass who is only unfoldin' one;
But she
Blessed wid all three—
Like my own Nora— Oh! *She* is the golden one.

Finer Clay

Sure, I used to think a pipe was the glory of a man,
   Troth I did then, Mary Ann.
Long before my years were ripe (wid a rattle in one han')
   I would smoke one, Mary Ann.
An', thinks I, there's nothin' gives
To the grandest man that lives
Such a finish, ye may say;
An' it's well I mind the way
That it nearly finished me.
But I wouldn't let it be
   Till I liked it, Mary Ann.

Then I found an ould dhudeen was a comfort to a man,
   An' none betther, Mary Ann;
For wid that my teeth between, if I'd work to do or plan,
   It was aisy, Mary Ann.
An' the more I smoked my clay,
All the more I worked away;
An' my thoughts were keen an' long
When the pipe was goin' strong.
For the two of us, ye see,
Were just suited to a "t"
   Wid each other, Mary Ann.

So the pipe became my all, an' meself, a lonely man,
   Grew to love it, Mary Ann.
But there's changes do befall that ye never un'erstan';
   Faith, they do, then, Mary Ann.
An' tonight there's somethin' wrong;
For I've sat here thinkin' long,

But my thoughts an' pipe don't fit,
For I cannot keep it lit.
What I'm tellin' ye is true,
An' the throuble, dear, is *you*—
  Sure, it's jealous, Mary Ann!

Cornaylius Ha-Ha-Ha-Hannigan

'Twas the godfather stuttered, or mayhap the priest;
But, be that as it may, it is certain, at least,
That the wan or the other was surely to blame
Fur presentin' the lad the quare twist to his name.
    For there at the christ'nin',
    Wid iv'rywan list'nin',
Now didn't his Riverence, Father O'Flanigan,
    Wid nervousness stam'rin',
    Bechune the child's clam'rin',
Baptize it "Cornaylius Ha-Ha-Ha-Hannigan?"

Wid these words from the priest, sure, the cute little rogue
Up an' stopped his own mouth wid his chubby kithogue,
An' the dimples broke out an' proceeded to chase
All the tears an' the frowns from his innocint face.
    For, faix, he was afther
    Absorbin' the laughther
Stuck into his name by good Father O'Flanigan!
    Now that's the truth in it,
    An' so from that minute
Sure, ev'rywan called the lad "Ha-Ha-Ha-Hannigan."

Now, the "ha! ha! ha!" stuck to him close as his name,
For the sorra a tear could be drownin' the same.
Not a care ever touched him from that blessid day
But his gift o' the laughther would drive it away.
    Wid jokin' an' chaffin'
    He never stopped laughin',
Or if he did stop he immajiate began agin;
    An' ev'rywan hearin'
    His laughther so cheerin'
Just j'ined in the mirth o' young "Ha-Ha-Ha-Hannigan."

Sure, the throubles o' life are so palthry an' small
'Tis a pity we let thim disturb us at all.
There is never a care but would l'ave us in p'ace
If we'd only stand up an' just laugh in its face.

    Faix, life were a pleasure
    If all had the treasure
Conferred so unthinkin' by Father O'Flanigan;
    If all could but borrow
    That cure-all for sorrow
Possissed by "Cornaylius Ha-Ha-Ha-Hannigan!"

The Mourner

Out o' bed of a mornin' was Mary McCroal
  Before ever a sunbeam had cut its first caper,
An' had fetched from her door-step her bit of a roll
  An' her wee jar o' milk an' her mornin' newspaper.
Then, the while she was wettin' her kittle o' tay,
  She'd the paper forninst her ould specks as she read
What she held "the importantest news o' the day"—
  An' that same was no more nor the list o' the dead.
She could aisily wait fur the bit an' the sup,
  But the hunger fur news she could never control,
Readin' wan colyume down an' the nixt colyume up,
  Till: "Here's wan at St. Ann's," cried ould Mary McCroal,
    "May the Lord rest his soul!"

She'd make way wid her tay in two minyutes or less,
  An' she'd ready the table an' lay the cloth on it,
An' she'd deck hersel' out in her dacint black dress
  An' her cashymere shawl an' her ould velvet bonnet.
Then 'twas off at a trot to the Church o' St. Ann—
  To be there when the corpse an' the mourners came in.
Sure, what odds if she never had heard o' the man,
  Nor had knowledge at all of a wan of his kin?
Faix, 'twas little, indeed, that the corpse needed care,
  An' no bar to his soul on the way to its goal,
If no wan o' the mourners there bowin' in prayer
  Prayed as strong or as long as ould Mary McCroal:
    "May the Lord rest his soul!"

Ye might canvass the parish; not wan on the list—
  Not a wan—but would tell ye he couldn't remember
Anny funeral Mass that she ever had missed,
  Under roses o' June or in snows o' December;

An' there's some that'd smile, recollectin' the sight
　　Of a red flannel petticoat, aye! an' a show
Of a dacint clane stockin', ould-fashioned an' white,
　　Whiskin' over the graves in the dust or the snow.
There was some might have said, wid a shake o' the head,
　　She was just an ould crow. But ye'd find, on the whole,
Not a wan o' thim all, when they buried their dead,
　　But was glad o' the prayers of ould Mary McCroal . . .
　　May the Lord rest her soul!

Aye! "the Lord rest *her* soul." Ah! the church was so bare
　　When she lay there th'-day, fur the mourners were few.
But, sure, why should she care that the only wans there
　　Were the sexton, the priest, an' ould woman or two?
An' what odds if the prayers at her passin' were brief
　　As the ride to the grave, when those prayers had been said?
An' what need was there here fur the trappin's o' grief?
　　Fur, sure, death was a joy to this friend o' the dead.
Ah! 'tis well to believe that the prayers that she prayed
　　Fur the many before her who shared of her dole,
They have gathered together an' woven an' made
　　As a ladder o' light fur ould Mary McCroal.
　　May the Lord rest her soul!

Cordaylia o' the Alley

At the corner o' the alley
  Sits Cordaylia McNally,
At the corner o' the alley where the people come an' go,
  In a penitent procession,
  Passin' to an' from confession
In the ould Church of St. Joseph that was builded long ago.
  Oh, 'tis well she knows there's many
  Has the charitable penny
More convaynient to their fingers then than any other day,
  An' her tongue it is so sooth'rin'
  An' so mastherful deludth'rin'
There are mortial few whatever she'll be lettin' get away.

For, oh, the Irish eyes of her
  They twinkle at ye so,
Ye hate to think the sighs of her
Are part o' the disguise of her,
  So, faix, she has yer penny gathered in before ye know.

  There's small use in walkin' fasther
  In the hope o' sneakin' past her,
Sure, she'll let ye go, unnoticed, wid yer little load o' sin.
  But, O! man, she has ye spotted,
  An' yer penny good as potted,
Fur she knows that ye'll be softer comin' out than goin' in!
  Fur there's nothin' but good nature
  In the m'anest Irish crayture
Whin he feels the soul inside o' him is cleansed of ev'ry blot.
  Should Cordaylia then address ye
  Wid her sootherin' "God bless ye!"
'Tis not you will dare to judge if she's deservin' it or not.

For, oh, the Irish eyes of her
  They twinkle at ye so,
Ye hate to think the sighs of her
Are part o' the disguise of her,
  So, faix, she has yer penny gathered in before ye know.

The Ould Apple Woman

Wid her basket of apples comes Nora McHugh,
   Wid her candies an' cakes an' wan thing an' another,
But the best thing she brings to commind her to you
   Is the smile in her eyes that no throuble can smother.
An' the wit that's at home in the tip of her tongue
   Has a freshness unknown to her candy and cake;
Though her wares had been stale since ould Nora was young,
   There is little complaint you'd be carin' to make.
Well I mind, on a day, I complained of a worm
   That I found in an apple, near bitten in two.
"But suppose ye had bit it, an' where'd be the harm?
   For, sure, this isn't Friday," said Nora McHugh.

O Nora McHugh, you've the blarneyin' twist in you,
Where is the anger could drame o' resistin' you?
   Faix, we'll be sp'ilin' you,
   Blind to the guile in you,
   While there's a smile in you,
      Nora McHugh.

It was Mistress De Vere, that's so proud of her name,
   Fell to boastin' wan day of her kin in the peerage—
Though there's some o' thim same, years ago whin they came
   To this glorious land, was contint wid the steerage—
An' she bragged of her ancistry, Norman an' Dane,
   An' the like furrin ancients that's thought to be swell.
"Now, I hope," said ould Nora, "ye'll not think me vain,
   Fur it's little I care fur ancistry mesel';
But wid all o' your pedigree, ma'am, I believe
   'Tis mesel' can go back a bit further than you,
Fur in me you perceive a descindant of Eve,
   The first apple woman," said Nora McHugh.

O Nora McHugh, sich owdacious frivolity!
How can you dare to be jokin' the quality?
  Still, we'll be sp'ilin' you,
  Blind to the guile in you,
  While there's a smile in you,
      Nora McHugh.

The Song of the Thrush

Ah! the May was grand this mornin'!
Sure, how could I feel forlorn in
Such a land, when tree and flower tossed their kisses to the
    breeze?
Could an Irish heart be quiet
While the spring was runnin' riot,
An' the birds of free America were singin' in the trees?
In the songs that they were singin'
No familiar note was ringin',
But I strove to imitate them an' I whistled like a lad.
Oh, my heart was warm to love them
For the very newness of them—
For the ould songs that they helped me to forget—an' I was glad.

So I mocked the feathered choir
To my hungry heart's desire,
An' I gloried in the comradeship that made their joy my own,
Till a new note sounded, stillin'
All the rest. A thrush was trillin'!
Ah! the thrush I left behind me in the fields about Athlone!
Where, upon the whitethorn swayin',
He was minstrel of the Mayin',
In my days of love an' laughter that the years have laid at rest;
Here again his notes were ringin'!
But I'd lost the heart for singin'—
Ah! the song I could not answer was the one I knew the best.

The Irish Bird-charmer

Wid more or less o' tuneful grace,
  As fits a Celtic singer,
I've praised the "great bird of our race,"
  The stork, the blessin'-bringer.
When first to my poor roof he came,
  How sweetly he was sung to!
I called him every dacint name
  That I could lay my tongue to.
But glory be! that praise from me
  So pleased the simple crayture
His visits here have come to be
  A sort o' second nature.
I'm glad to see him now an' then,
  But, glory be to Heaven!
If here he isn't back again,
  An' this is number seven!

Och! though this gift o' song may be
  In manny ways a blessin',
It brings some popularity
  That gets to be disthressin'.
Now, mind, I love this Irish bird—
  We couldn't live widout him—
An', sure, I'll not take back a word
  I ever said about him,
But now when all these mouths to feed
  Ate up our little savin's,
The birds whose visits most we need
  Are ould Elijah's ravens.
Begor'! if *they* were 'round these days
  An' I could make them hear me,
I'd sing them such a song o' praise
  'Twould keep them always near me.

The Peaceable Race

"Who says that the Irish are fighters be birth?"
        Says little Dan Crone.
"Faix, there's not a more peaceable race on th' earth,
        If ye l'ave 'em alone.

"Tim O'Toole? Well, I grant ye now, there is a lad
That's beset wid the curse o' pugnacity bad,
But he's just th' exciption that's provin' the rule;
An' what else could ye ask from a lad like O'Toole?
Sure, he's sich a big mountain o' muscle and bone,
Sizin' up to the heft o' some siventeen stone,
That he fair aggravates ev'ry other bould buck
To be wishful to thump him a little for luck,
An' to prove that there's others as clever as him.
Now, I ask ye, suppose ye was sturdy as Tim,
Don't ye think 'twould be right ye should take a delight
In defindin' yer title an' testin' yer might?"
        Says little Dan Crone.

"Is it me? Arrah! now it is jokin' ye are.
But I bid ye be careful an' not go too far.
Sure, it's true I'm no more nor the height o' yer waist,
But there's manny a bigger has sampled a taste
O' the knuckles that's bunched in this little ould fisht.
Where's the dog wouldn't fight whin his tail gets a twisht?
Do I hunt fur the throuble? Mayhap, now, it's thrue
Upon certain occasions that's just what I do.
Sure, how else would they know—I'm that stunted an' small—
I'd the heart of a man in me body at all?"
        Says little Dan Crone.

123

"Well, then, keep yer opinion. 'Tis little it's worth,"
  Says little Dan Crone.
"Faix, we're just the most peaceable race on the earth,
  If ye l'ave us alone."

Applying the Sermon

"O the pastor'd a sermon was splendid this mornin',"
        Said Nora O'Hare,
"But there's some in the parish that must have had warnin'
        An' worshiped elsewhere;
But wherever they were, if their ears wasn't burnin',
        Troth, then, it is quare!"

" 'There are women,' sez he, 'an' they're here in this parish,
        An' plentiful, too,
Wid their noses so high an' their manners so airish,
        But virtues so few
'Tis a wonder they can't see how much they resemble
        The proud Pharisee.
Ye would think they'd look into their own souls an' tremble
        Such sinners to be.
Not at all! They believe themselves better than others,
        An' give themselves airs
Till the pride o' them strangles all virtues, an' smothers
        The good o' their prayers.'

"That's the way he wint at them, an', faith, it was splendid—
        But wasted, I fear,
Wid the most o' the women for whom 'twas intended,
        Not there for to hear.
An' thinks I to meself, walkin' home, what a pity
        That Mary Ann Hayes
An' Cordelia McCann should be out o' the city
        This day of all days.

"But, indeed, 'twas a glorious sermon this mornin',"
        Said Nora O'Hare,

"Though I'm sorry that some o' the parish had warnin'
      An' worshiped elsewhere;
But wherever they were, if their ears wasn't burnin',
      Troth, then, it is quare!"

Two Days

Old Mike Clancy went for a stroll,
  An' warm an' clear was the sky,
But he came back home with clouds on his soul
  An' a glint o' rain in his eye.

"Och! cold it is out there," sez he;
"The street's no place these days fur me;
Wid motors runnin' through the town
The way they're like to knock ye down,
Wid all the rush an' moidherin' noise,
The impudence of upstart boys,
An' girls, that walk as bold as brass,
An' l'ave small room fur ye to pass.
In twenty blocks, or mebbe more,
I saw no face I'd seen before,
Or care, indeed, to see agen!
W'at's come of all the dacint men,
The kindly friends, I use' to meet
In other days upon the street?
'Tis here at home's the place fur me;
Och! cold it is out there," sez he.

Old Mike Clancy went for a stroll,
  An' cold an' gray was the sky,
But he came back home with warmth in his soul
  An' a glint o' sun in his eye.

"O! sure, this day was fine," sez he,
"An' who d'ye think walked up to me?
A man I thought long dead—Tim Kane!
Och! didn't we talk, there in the rain,

The soft, kind rain we use' to know—
O! not so very long ago—
An' didn't we have a dale to say?
He's eighty-two years old come May—
An' I'm no more than sivinty-nine!
An' didn't he stan' there straight an' fine?
It done me good, the look in his eye,
An' how he laughed an' slapped his thigh;
'I'm good,' sez he, 'fur ten years, too!'
An' faith I do believe it's true.
A man's as old as he feels, d'ye see?—
O! sure, this day was fine," sez he.

The Man's the Man

"The man's the man!" my Barney says—
  An' Barney's newly married—
"He's the wan that knows the ways
  The burdens should be carried.
Let the woman wear the grace
  An' pleasin' pranks o' beauty,
Yet be mindful of her place
  An' of her wifely duty;
By the crown within my hat,
  The chief of all our riches,
I'll be king o' this an' that;
  An' sure I'll wear the breeches;
Yes, an' need be, I can teach
  The 'Spanish way' o' walkin'!"
There's my Barney's manful speech—
  I listen to him talkin'.

"The man's the man!" my Barney says,
  An', faith, my thoughts are carried
Back to well-remembered days
  When I was newly married;
An' there's wan that's lookin' down
  Upon this house this minute,
Knows who was it wore the crown
  The while herself was in it.
Dull I was, but plain as day
  'Tis now I'm seein' through it
How she let me have *her* way,
  An' sure I never knew it;
Puffed wid pride as I could be
  An' struttin' 'round an' squawkin',
"Man's the man!" sez I, an' she—
  She listened to me talkin'.

April

April,
Irish through and through,
Here's my caubeen off to you!
Look you! now my head is bare,
Drop your tears upon my hair.
Weep your fill upon me, then
Warm me with your sun again.
Here's my heart. O! make its strings
Populous with linnets' wings.
So your holy birds are there
Not a ha'porth do I care;
Mute with sorrow, wild with glee,
So they make their home in me.

April,
Dead, forgotten days
Tremble in your dim blue haze;
All the glories of the race
Flicker on your mobile face.
Heroes panoplied for fight
Glimmer in your golden light;
Martyrs, sanctified by pain,
Murmur in your silver rain.
All your smiles and all your tears
Voicing now our hopes and fears,
April, Irish through and through,
Here's my caubeen off to you!

An Interparochial Affair

Och! there's divil a parish at all
Like this one o' St. Paul.
Here the winter begins wid the fall
An' it sticks to the middle o' May.
Streets an' houses an' people are gray,
An' the night lends its hue to the day;
For the blessed sun's light hangs like fog on the walls
Where a man does be livin' his lone in St. Paul's.

Faith, 'tis odd that the same parish plan
Gave so much to St. Ann.
There's one parish that's fit for a man
Wid a hunger for warmth an' for light!
'Tis a comfort to find, day an' night,
Streets an' houses an' people so bright;
For there's summer-warm hearts an' there's kind, open han's,
An' a girl wid a face like a rose, in St. Ann's.

In a parish just over the line,
Called St. John the Divine,
There's a cozy new cot, an' it's mine!
Oh! 'tis I will have throuble to hide
From my face all the joy an' the pride
That my heart will be feelin' inside,
When next Sunday at Mass they'll be readin' the banns
For meself o' St. Paul's and Herself o' St. Ann's.

The End o' the Day

Here's the end o' the day,
  An' this weary ould planet
Turns again to the gray,
  Dewy dusk that began it.
An' meself that's no more
  Nor a midge or a flea
Or a sand o' the shore,
  Who'd be thinkin' o' me
    At the end o' the day?

Here's the end o' the day,
  An' it's little I'm winnin'
Wid my toilin' away
  Since the same was beginnin';
But for all I'm so small,
  Trudgin' on by my lone,
If no evil befall
  I've a world o' my own
    At the end o' the day.

Here's the end o' the day,
  An' the stars, growin' bolder,
Now the sun is away,
  Peep above the hill's shoulder;
An' 'tis they that can see
  That the dusty boreen
Is a king's road for me
  To my castle an' queen,
    At the end o' the day.

The Whisperers

Look at ould Mag Carmody an' Anastasia Moore,
  Sittin' in the corner wid their elbows on their knees;
Wid their bony backs bent over an' their worn hands clasped
    before,
    An' the two white heads together like a pair o' buzzin' bees.
Wasps, more like, you'd call them, for the talk your fancy hears
  Passin' now between them wid a sting in every word,
Talk, ye think, would have the neighbors tinglin' at the ears,
  Wid the heat of anger an' resentment if they heard.
          So, if you'd your way,
          Faith, belike, you'd say:
        "Rise up, whisp'rin' gossips, rise!
          L'ave your scandals an' your lies;
Time enough for bitterness when wintry days befall.
          But the year is at the spring,
          Joy an' kindness are a-wing;
Even wasps are Mayin' now upon the sunny wall."

Look upon the whisperers again—an' hang yer head;
  Look upon them kindly, for not long you'll know their
    likes.
These are of the troublous days whose whisperin' was bred
  By the roar o' tyrant guns an' clash o' patriot pikes.
Innocent an' simple is the talk that now they make,
  Chat of olden buried things, for thoughts of age are long.
They've no need to whisper, still a habit's hard to break,
  An' wid two to nurse the same, sure they keep it strong.
          So, if you'd be kind,
          Thus you'll speak your mind:
        "Rise up, dear ould women, rise!
          Here you're under friendly skies;

Come an' take your fill o' talk an' share the genial sun.
      Here the year is at the spring,
      Joy and kindness are a-wing;
Come, forget the bitterness o' days that's dead an' done."

The Irish Genealogist

At wakes ye'll find her. Though, 'tis true,
They don't wake like they used to do,
There's still occasions when the clans
      Foregather,
An' there they'll sit wid folded han's,
      An' blather
Of this one's goodness, that one's sin,
Of this one's kith an' that one's kin—
Och! then, as soon as they begin
On intricate relationships,
She has 'em at her finger-tips.

  "His uncle on his mother's side
  Was John Cornaylius McBride,
  Whose cousin, Nora Flanagan,
  Half-sister to Kate Branigan,
  Who married an O'Hannigan—
    Not Malachi, but Tim—
  Was gran'son to that Matt Malone
  Whose cousin was a Kane, an' own
    Great-gran'mother to him!"

An' weddin's! Troth, ye'll find her there;
She'll make your brain more mixed an' quare
Than if ye'd take an' drain the bowl
      O' toddy;
Her talk would fair enslave your soul
      An' body.
No math'matician o' the schools,
Wid all his books an' all his rules,
Could folly her, when she be's-gin

To weave her tales o' kith an' kin;
An' here's the way she'll drag 'em in:

"Oh, isn't she the lovely bride?
I mind upon her father's side,
Her gran'aunt, Rose O'Rafferty,
First wife o' Larry Lafferty,
Was cousin to Grace Cafferty
    That married Phelim Burr.
An' he had copper kind o' hair
Which must explain, I do declare,
    The way it comes to her!"

In Praise of St. Stephen

Here's the feast o' St. Stephen,
  This Christmas Day's morrow,
An' it's past all believin'
  The comfort I borrow
      At the thought of him there
      In the cold mornin' air,
An' meself steppin' back to a world full o' sorrow.

For with all the soft beauty
  O' Christmas behind ye,
When it's back to cold duty
  This day has consigned ye,
      Faith, there's need of the aid
      Of a saint unafraid
To withstand the blue devils that's likely to find ye.

Tall and bright is the miter
  O' Stephen, the martyr;
A knight and a fighter
  By Christ the Lord's charter.
      And it's well if ye stand
      Within touch of his hand
In a world that is given to traffic and barter.

Lucky you, if ye're wearin'
  This saint's nomenclature,
For, belike, ye'll be sharin'
  His valorous nature;
      For there's none of his name
      In the pages o' fame
That was anything less than a two-fisted crayture.

137

So upon this gray mornin',
　　In hope o' receivin'
His good help in the scornin'
　　O' groanin' and grievin',
　　　　Here's the ballad I raise
　　　　In the merited praise
Of the worshipful martyr and fighter, St. Stephen!

A LA FRANCAISE

Ballade, by a Glutton

'Tis time to sing the joys of spring,
  So, come, my Muse, while I indite
A song of green things blossoming
  That put the winter's blues to flight—
  And here's a color-blend that might
Be cited now for highest praise—
  The green and gold of my delight—
Asparagus, with Hollandaise!

My soul is glad for everything
  That April brings—the mornings bright,
The buds, the robins' carolling—
  And yet, when I kneel down at night,
  I always think, in wild affright:
Suppose the sun too hot should blaze,
  Or killing frosts at night should blight
Asparagus, with Hollandaise!

Though California trains might bring
  Some sort of "grass" to ease our plight,
It's not the stuff of which I sing.
  The only "grass" that I invite
  To satisfy my appetite
Is what our nearby farmers raise—
  No other dish, indeed, is quite
Asparagus, with Hollandaise.

ENVOY

Dear Host (I say to every wight
  Who takes me out to lunch—and pays)
Whatever else you order, write:
  "Asparagus, with Hollandaise."

141

A Ballade of Brides

For brides who grace these passing days,
　　The poets lyric garlands twine;
For them the twittering song of praise
　　Resounds with many a fulsome line.
　　And unproved worth, as half divine,
Is glorified in tinkling tunes.
　　But worthier dames shall bless our wine—
We'll toast the brides of other Junes!

What though a thoughtless public pays
　　Its homage at young Beauty's shrine,
And wreathes smooth brows with orange sprays,
　　With roses and with eglantine,
　　Youth's cheeks that glow and eyes that shine
Are not the most enduring boons.
　　O! we who've seen such things decline,
We'll toast the brides of other Junes!

Though flowery wreaths and poets' lays
　　To grace the new-made bride combine,
O! let us rather twine the bays
　　For tried and true ones, thine and mine,
　　Who share whate'er the fates design
To bless or blight our nights and noons;
　　Good comrades still through rain or shine—
We'll toast the brides of other Junes!

ENVOY

Old Friend! whose bride of Auld Lang Syne
　　Still fills thy life with honeymoons,
Thy glass to mine, my glass to thine—
　　We'll toast the brides of other Junes!

Ballade of Summer's Passing

Like a matron grown jaded—
 Fat, forty and fair—
In a nook cool and shaded,
 Who nods in her chair;
 Then, sudden, aware
Of the eyes of the masses,
 Feigns a wide-awake air,
Summer smiles as she passes.

All the charms she paraded
 In Junetime so rare,
When new roses were braided
 And twined in her hair,
 No longer are there.
All her gold but worn brass is,
 But, still debonair,
Summer smiles as she passes.

That her beauty is faded
 Beyond all repair,
All the pools where she waded—
 Her mirrors declare.
 Brown limbs that are bare
Every woodland pool glasses;
 But what does she care?
Summer smiles as she passes.

ENVOY

Come, then, Autumn! and dare
 To be brave as this lass is,
When the like fate you share—
 Summer smiles as she passes.

143

Roundel by a Rounder

Beach censorship, the local authorities declare, will not be so
strict this season. At least, no special attention will be paid to
what women wear.
                                                —Atlantic City despatch.

What women wear, in mid-July
   On bathing beaches, who will care?
We've ceased to try to rectify
   What women wear.

And yet, if—from my rolling-chair—
   I heard somebody passing by
Say: "Look at those bold women there!"
   I'm very much afraid that I
Would rise on tippy-toes to stare,
   And you might hear my eager cry:
   "What women? Where?"

Ballade of the Tempting Book

Sometimes when I sit down at night
  And try to think of something new,
Some odd conceit that I may write
  And work into a verse or two,
  There often dawns upon my view,
The while my feeble thoughts I nurse,
  A little book in gold and blue—
"The Oxford Book of English Verse."

And though I try, in wild affright
  At thought of all I have to do,
To keep that volume out of sight,
  If I so much as look askew
  I catch it playing peek-a-boo.
Then work may go to—pot, or worse!
  I'm giving up the evening to
"The Oxford Book of English Verse."

O! some for essays recondite,
  And some for frothy fiction sue,
But give to me for my delight
  One tuneful tome to ramble through;
  To hear the first quaint "Sing Cuccu!"
And all those noble songs rehearse
  Whose deathless melodies imbue
"The Oxford Book of English Verse."

ENVOY

Kind Reader, here's a tip for you:
  Go buy, though skinny be your purse
And other books of yours be few,
  "The Oxford Book of English Verse."

Cherry Pie

O cherry pie! A song for thee!
Let not the crusts close-wedded be,
  But puffed and flaky, plumped with meat,
  And all the red heart dripping sweet
With luscious oozings syrupy.

Ah! that's the cherry pie for me!
I'll want two "helpin's"; maybe three—
  Who ever got enough to eat
      O' cherry pie?

What odds if in our dreams we see
Nightmares and goblins? We'll agree,
  Though Pain usurp Joy's earlier seat,
  No collywobs can quite defeat
The gustatory pleasures we
     Owe cherry pie.

Pity the Poor Poet

The poet burns, the whole night through,
His "midnight oil," to weave a few
  Fresh-fashioned stanzas, grave or gay,
  Which in the public prints next day
May earn a word of praise from you.

'Tis not an easy thing to do,
When thoughts go lame and rhymes askew;
  So, many an imperfect lay
      The poet burns.

Small wonder if, for cheer, he brew
That "bracer" (this may be untrue;
  I only quote what people say)
  Which once drove carking care away
And brought such inspiration to
      The poet Burns.

Ballade to the Women

The poets, extolling the graces
  Of sweet femininity, pay
Particular court, in most cases,
  To Phyllis or Phoebe or Fay.
  "A toast to the ladies!" they say—
As "ladies" they always address them—
  And bid us bow down to them. Nay!
We sing the plain "women," God bless them!

Though light-o'-loves, frail as the laces
  And satins in which they array
The charms of their forms and their faces,
  Are "ladies" for their little day,
  The feet of such idols are clay.
Our wives, when we come to possess them,
  Must loom to us larger than they.
We sing the plain "women," God bless them!

Sweet creatures who make the home-places
  As cheerful and bright as they may,
Whose feminine beauty embraces
  A heart to illumine the way,
  Though skies may be ever so gray;
Good mothers, whose children caress them
  And hail them as chums at their play—
We sing the plain "women," God bless them!

ENVOY

O! Queen, teach the "ladies," we pray,
  Whenever vain notions oppress them,
Though idly their charms we survey,
  We sing the plain "women," God bless them!

Ballade of Those Present

To the papers whose trade is supplying
    The news in a gossipy way,
All the workaday world should be hieing,
    Its compliments grateful to pay.
    How kind to the public are they
When they publish our names in their pleasant
    Descriptions of ball or soirée
As "among the most prominent present!"

When we sit at the banquet board, trying
    To tickle our palates blasé,
Comes a thought that is more gratifying
    Than all the Lucullan array;
    More sweet than the sherry's bouquet,
Or the flavor of succulent pheasant—
    The thought of appearing next day
As "among the most prominent present."

Since the common folk simply are dying
    To know what we do or we say,
It were really a shame our denying
    To them all the pleasure we may.
    Then the news let the papers convey
To the shopman, mechanic and peasant,
    Noting *us* at the dance or the play
As "among the most prominent present."

ENVOY

St. Peter, receive us, we pray,
    When we've done with this world evanescent,
Assigning us places for aye
    As "among the most prominent present."

149

Hearts Apart

To count the days until we twain
May read each other's eyes again,
  And dwell once more in Arcady,
  Is all my joy away from thee—
Is all my joy and all my pain.

When leaden-footed minutes wane
To hours that burden heart and brain,
  'Twere but a useless agony
      To count the days,
Did thy most gracious heart not deign
To bid my own heart entertain
  The hope of better things to be;
  Did I not know thy constancy
And that, until we meet again.
      Two count the days.

Mistletoe and Holly

The mistletoe is gemmed with pearls,
  Red berries hath the holly.
Remember, all ye modest girls,
The mistletoe is gemmed with pearls,
And when it hangs above your curls,
  Away with melancholy!
The mistletoe is gemmed with pearls,
  Red berries hath the holly.

Since mistletoe is hard to find,
  We do not need it, Mollie.
O! do, I beg of you, be kind;
Since mistletoe is hard to find,
Pretend that you are color-blind
  And kiss beneath this holly.
Since mistletoe is hard to find,
  We do not need it, Mollie.

At Home

At home tonight, alone with Dot,
I rest my soul and care not what
  In worlds beyond may come or go.
  Four walls, a roof, to brave the snow,
Suffice to bound this Eden spot.

Dot has her sewing things; I've got
My pipe, a glass of something hot
  And Dot herself. The world's aglow,
    At home tonight.

As lovers in some golden plot
The poet weaves of Camelot,
  We feel apart from earth. We know
  The servant in the hall below
Will say to all who call we're not
    At home tonight.

Ballade of Sportsmanship

You put your prowess to the test,
  In whatsoever wholesome play,
And wearing Honor, like a crest,
  Aloft and stainless through the fray,
  Press on with valor. Come what may,
Shall Justice grant you, or refuse,
  Full credit or full debit? Nay,
You share the laurels, win or lose!

You, Champion, who, with heaving breast,
  Received the plaudits and the bay,
How much you owe, were all confessed,
  To him that, like a shadow gray,
  Pursued and spurred but could not stay
The triumph of your straining thews!
  May we not, therefore, justly say
You share the laurels, win or lose?

And what of those, unseen, who pressed
  About your goal-line? Are not they,
Who watched you giving of your best,
  Those victors of an earlier day,
  Your sharers, since they blazed the way?
And he who failed, yet scorned the ruse,
  This unction to his soul may lay:
You share the laurels, win or lose.

Good Sportsmen all! Time cannot sway
  This strict adjustment of the dues;
Vanquished and victors get, and pay—
  You share the laurels, win or lose.

Ballade of the News

We scribbling toilers of the press,
  Who tell each day, who's who, what's what,
Admit the tedious tawdriness
  Of all we weave into the plot.
  There's much of it we'd like to blot,
But may not tamper with the text,
  And each day's grimy grist has got
To be continued in our next.

Our serial's a dismal mess
  Of Pollyanna, polyglot,
Plain bunk, a smile or two, distress,
  Raw sin, fool pride and all that rot.
  We serve it to you piping hot,
And, though your stomach's sore perplexed,
  There'll still be plenty in the pot
To be continued in our next.

From day to day we cannot guess,
  Nor change the bill-of-fare one jot.
Thus run the items, more or less:
  "Bold Bandits Steal a Private Yacht,"
  "More Bootleg Graft," "Two Gunmen Shot,"
"Poor Underfed, Rich Oversexed,"
  "Speed Demon Slays a Tiny Tot"—
To be continued in our next.

ENVOY

But peace, Dear Reader! Though our lot
  In this life is so sadly vexed,
We're pretty well assured 'tis not
  To be continued in our next.

The Fare in Lent

The fare in Lent should be austere.
No cakes and ale, no kraut and beer;
   No fatted goose, with heavy wines,
   That Croesus fancies when he dines—
They're all taboo this time o' year.

Particularly you, my dear,
Should lend at least one pearly ear
   To every dictum that defines
      The fare in Lent.

For you, who are so full of fear
Your girlish form will disappear,
   Just think how Lent's austere designs
   Will help you hold your sylph-like lines!
Indeed, the prospect ought to cheer
      The fair, in Lent.

The Tides of Love

Flo was fond of Ebenezer—
  "Eb," for short, she called her beau.
Talk of Tides of Love, great Caesar!
  You should see them—Eb and Flo.

From an Attic Window

She lives in the square below me there.
  Ah! me, if she'd only love me!
She lives in the square below me there,
  But moves in a circle above me.

A Song to One

If few are won to read my lays
And offer me a word of praise,
  If there are only one or two
  To take my rhymes and read them through,
I may not claim the poet's bays.

I care not, when my Fancy plays
Its one sweet note, if it should raise
  A host of listeners or few—
     If you are one.

The homage that my full heart pays
To Womanhood in divers ways,
  Begins and ends, my love, in you.
  My lines may halt, but strong and true
My soul shall sing through all its days,
     If you are won.

ANGLICE

For Old Lovers

The sap is bubbling in the tree,
   The pink buds herald spring.
Yet winter holds for you and me
   One charm to which we cling.
The April sun grows warm by noon,
   Its daylight skies are bright;
But the cool evenings bring the boon
   Of a wood fire at night.

The greening sod of April days
   Is lovely to the eye,
But firmer, lovelier turf is May's
   And kindlier glows the sky.
Let striplings to the greenwood go
   For April's chill delight,
But we two still shall bless the glow
   Of a wood fire at night.

To a Violinist

Applause! A rapturous burst
Spreads downward from the gods, who see you first
As you come bouncing in,
A little fat, unconscious harlequin. . . .
Clutching your fiddle in your hand,
Now in midstage you stand,
Bobbing and bowing, stiffly, jerkily,
  To left, to right, to left,
    And never for a moment still.
We, in the stalls, we smile to see
  How droll you look; and even when your deft,
    Quick fingers rouse the charm'd strings to your will,
    The laughter, lurking in our lashes still,
Beats back the elfin voices at our ears.

How like a boat your violin appears
As, under lowered lids, our listless eyes
Watch its alternate rise and fall and rise,
Where, as the music sways, it seems to be
Tossed by the tempests on a fairy sea. . . .
And this strange sense, this sense of finer air
That, like a tide at flood, is everywhere,
Bearing up from depths unfathomed voices long imprisoned
        there,
Voices of the singing birds that flattered unto happy tears
Lovers lingering in the twilights of how many thousand years!
Voices moaning and intoning of old sorrows, hopes and fears!
Sounds of waves on craggy beaches and of winds that shout
        above,
Melting, dwindle to a murmur, like the cooing of the dove,
Rise again and, waxing stronger, swell into a chant of love.

Round and round the waves of music sweep through this en-
chanted place,
Catch the souls come forth to listen, trembling on each hearer's
face,
Draw them on and whirl them swiftly, lightly through the fields
of space,
Till the music and its maker and the hearers are as one—
And the masterwork is done!

> Applause, spontaneous, springs,
> Pursues you to the wings
> And hales you out once more.
> Encore! Encore! Encore!
> Come back and bow, bow, bow—
> You are not comic now.

The Day of the Circus Horse

It was a fiery circus horse
  That ramped and stamped and neighed,
Till every creature in its course
  Fled, frightened and dismayed.
The chickens on the roadway's edge
  Arose, and flapped their wings,
And making for the sheltering hedge
  Flew off like crazy things.

Nor iron gates nor fences barred
  That mettled steed's career.
It galloped right across our yard
  And filled us all with fear;
And when it tossed its head and ran
  Straight through the pantry door,
Cook almost dropped her frying-pan
  Upon the kitchen floor!

It neighed and pranced and wheeled about
  And scampered off, but then
We scarcely saw the creature out
  When it was in again.
And so throughout the livelong day,
  Through house and yard and street,
That charger held its fearsome way
  And only stopped to eat.

But when, at dusk, a little lame,
  It slowly climbed the stairs,
Behold! a gentle lady came
  And made it say its prayers.

Now, what a wondrous change you see!
  'Sh! Come and take a peep—
Here lies, as tame as tame can be,
  A little boy, asleep!

Along the Wissahickon

The red and gold and silver haze
Of early Indian summer days
    Along the Wissahickon!
Dan Cupid, could there ever be
A likelier place on land or sea
Wherein to plan your Arcady
    And let your love plots thicken?
There earliest stirred the feet of spring,
There summer dreamed on drowsy wing!
And autumn's glories longest cling
    Along the Wissahickon.

On winter nights ghost-music plays
(The bells of long-forgotten sleighs)
    Along the Wissahickon,
And many a silver-headed wight
Who drove that pleasant road by night
Sighs now for his old appetite
    For waffles hot and chicken.
And grandmas now, who then were belles!
How many a placid bosom swells
At thought of love's old charms and spells
    Along the Wissahickon.

You, Gloriana, you who know
The word, low spoken long ago,
    Along the Wissahickon,
The word that was the golden key
To ope the gates of Arcady
For one man. Come! and walk with me
    Where sweetest memories quicken,

That once again the charms that brood
Through all the sylvan solitude
May bless the wooer and the wooed—
    Along the Wissahickon.

In Praise of Scrapple

Out upon your gibes ironic!
You who've never known the tonic
  Toothsomeness of savory scrapple
Dare to judge it? Well, I never!
When no morsel of it ever
  Greased your graceless Adam's apple.

When the northwest wind is blowing,
Sharp enough for frost or snowing,
And the days of muggy weather
Have departed altogether,
All our husbandmen are getting
Butcher knives laid out for whetting,
And some morning with the dawn
Comes the porcine slaughter on.
Let's not morbidly be dealing
With the scuffling and the squealing,
But, the gruesome parts deleting,
Get us to the joys of eating.
Well, then, when hog-killing's through
This is what the housewives do:
Clean a pig's head, nicely, neatly,
Boil till meat leaves bones completely,
When it's cold remove all greases,
Chop meat into little pieces;
Put the liquor and the meat
Back again upon the heat,
Slowly stirring cornmeal in
Till it is no longer thin.
Pepper, salt and sage then bring
For its proper seasoning.

When the mess is thick and hot
It is lifted from the pot,
Poured then into pans to mold
And so left until it's cold.
So ends Chapter I.
                    The sequel
Is a breakfast without equal!

Come! it is a nippy morning,
Frosty lace, the panes adorning,
Takes the sun from many angles
And the windows glow with spangles.
From the kitchen range are rising
Odors richly appetizing;
Paradise is in the skillet,
For the scrapple slices fill it,
And each flour-encrusted piece
Smiling in its fragrant grease
Takes a coat of golden tan
From the ardor of the pan.
Crisp and brown the outer crust, oh!
Food to rouse the gourmand's gusto
From your platter gives you greeting;
Truly this is royal eating!

Out upon your gibes ironic!
You who've never known the tonic
    Toothsomeness of savory scrapple,
Dare to judge it? Well, I never!
May no morsel of it ever
    Grease your graceless Adam's apple!

What the Farmer Saw

John D.
Rockefeller, he
Seemed as pleased as pleased could be.
Seen him stop, stoop down an' pass
Long lean fingers through the grass,
Pull 'em out an' smile a smile
Slick as his own Standard Ile;
Them long fingers seemed to hold
Somethin' precious, mebbe gold—
      Anyways,
John D.
Rockefeller, he
Seemed as pleased as pleased could be.

Seen him shake his head an' stand
With the treasure in his hand,
Gloatin' on it, figgerin' out
What his find was worth, no doubt,
Turnin' of it 'round and 'round—
Must 'a' been a pearl he'd found—
      Anyways,
John D.
Rockefeller, he
Seemed as pleased as pleased could be.

Snuck up closer, as I passed;
Seen jist what it was at last
That had tickled of him so;
Looked an' seen it plain, but sho!
Blamed thing wusn't much at all—
Nothin' but a golf-game ball!

        An' yit
John D.
Rockefeller, he
Seemed as pleased as pleased could be.

A Valentine

There was a time, when we were young together
  And all the thorns of life were yet to seek,
This day brought roses, in the wintriest weather,
  To burn your cheek.

Oh, not alone the wanton winds that sought you
  Were wont your lilies to incarnadine;
Your roses deepened when the postman brought you
  My valentine.

The words I wrote, my still fond breast remembers,
  Were leaping tongues from out a heart of fire;
They breathed, nor have they lost in graying embers,
  Young love's desire!

But now, my dear, this fervent song I sing you
  Has holier designs on heaven's wealth;
I pray this little valentine may bring you
  The rose of health.

The Journey's End

Good-bye, dear heart. Be thou, as I am, glad.
  Glad for the grace of loneliness and yearning
My heart, far faring from thee, shall have had
  Ere its returning.
Pluck future joy from out this present pain;
  Rejoice to know that these small seeds of sorrow
Shall be Love's harvest when we meet again,
  Some bright tomorrow.

Flag o' My Land

Up to the breeze of the morning I fling you,
  Blending your folds with the dawn in the sky;
There let the people behold you, and bring you
  Love and devotion that never shall die.
    Proudly, agaze at your glory, I stand,
    Flag o' my land! flag o' my land!

Standard most glorious! banner of beauty!
  Whither you beckon me there will I go,
Only to you, after God, is my duty;
  Unto no other allegiance I owe.
    Heart of me, soul of me, yours to command,
    Flag o' my land! flag o' my land!

Pine to palmetto and ocean to ocean,
  Though of strange nations we get our increase,
Here are your worshipers one in devotion,
  Whether the bugles blow battle or peace.
    Take us and make us your patriot band,
    Flag o' my land! flag o' my land!

Now to the breeze of the morning I give you—
  Ah! but the days when the staff will be bare!
Teach us to see you and love you and live you
  When the light fades and your folds are not there.
    Dwell in the hearts that are yours to command,
    Flag o' my land! flag o' my land!

The Magic Apple

"A thing of beauty is a joy forever."
Though years becloud it, never may they sever
Its lovely essence utterly from earth;
Never a joy was born but hath rebirth.
There was a sunset lost, long, long ago,
   An autumn sunset seen through orchard boughs.
A boy's eye brightening in the amber glow
   Gave to his mind no more of it to house
For the delight of manhood's pensive days
Than the bare memory of time and place;
      So nigh forgot, it seemed
      As something he had dreamed.
Yet now the man, before whose boyish ken
   The glory melted on the evening breeze,
Knows it lived on, for he hath found again
   His long-lost sunset of the orchard trees.

A penny tribute to a swarthy vendor
Hath filled for me this city street with splendor.
A meagre apple! yet its crushed pulp drips
A long-forgotten savor on my lips,
A rare, faint essence tasted once before,
   But only once; and suddenly I find
The honeyed gush hath loosed a long-locked door,
   And all the olden splendor floods my mind.
      A care-free lad I stand,
      An apple in my hand,
And watch the amber glory grow and wane.
   I feel upon my cheek the evening breeze.
Joy lives forever! I have found again
   My long-lost sunset of the orchard trees!

175

October Song in Romany

Mother and wife to me,
    Fostering Earth!
Sum of all life to me,
    Birth to rebirth;
Mother, at urge of the sun-god who bore me,
Wife, whose cool bosom at last shall swell o'er me,
    Ever and ever my heart shall be thine.
Ah! but one season brings *thy* heart the nearest,
When to my loving thy bosom thou barest.
    Then thou art mine.

Summer brings many men
    Singing thy praise,
But are there any when
    Chill are the days?
Now, when thy robes are but tatters and patches,
Sport of the winds in the bitter night watches,
    Stronger and truer my heart beats to thine.
My breast to thine and the deep sky our cover,
Quiet and peace for the loved and the lover—
    Now thou art mine!

What the Flag Sings

My People! ye who honor me,
Upon this day that made ye free,
And for your badge of liberty
    On high have set me,
Hear what my breeze-tossed ripples say,
Ere with the passing of this day
I once again am put away
    And ye forget me:

"In war begot, by war imbrued
Baptismally with patriot blood,
Triumphant, steadfast still, through good
    And evil omen,
I've watched victorious Peace alight
Upon the arms of Truth and Right,
Which nevermore shall fear the might
    Of foreign foemen.

"But, O! my people, help me preach
Our gospel now, that we may teach
Newcomers here of alien speech
    To know and love me.
Teach that the cause for which I stand,
The liberty of this fair land,
Will tolerate no Anarch brand
    To float above me.

"Aye! our own native faults lay bare!
Point out the specious statesman's snare,
Whose tongue would hide with shout and prayer
    His heart's sedition;

177

Who lifts to me his crafty eyes
And breathes abroad his soulful sighs,
Which not from love of me arise,
     But low ambition.

"O! teach and learn! And when the sky
This day's departing sunbeams dye,
And from the staff whereon I fly
     At last ye take me,
Remember what ye owe to me;
I'm but your *badge* of liberty,
And I no greater thing can be
     Than your deeds make me!"

July 4, 1912

The Fallen Tree

There was a tree in Wister Wood
  Last April's livery wore
Of emerald leaf and crimson bud,
  But it is there no more.

There, earliest, on twig and bough,
  I marked the spring's advance;
Of all who note its absence now
  I only care, perchance.

Yet 'tis enough. For ne'er, for me,
  Shall any spring come in
But all its trees shall lovelier be
  Because this one hath been.

So may it be with me, whose blood
  Stirs ever when the spring
Calls out to me from Wister Wood
  And bids me rise and sing.

Enough for me, if when I've gone
  The way of man and tree,
Some spring be made more sweet for one,
  Through kindly thought of me.

To the Joy-bringer

Happy, together we have watched our boys
  At merrymaking, by the summer sea,
  In autumn woods, beneath our own roof-tree,
Nor ever wished to draw them from their toys
For formal thanks to us; for through the noise
  Of their rough play and fresh, unfettered glee
  Rang praise enough, dear heart, for thee and me,
Who, under God, are makers of their joys.

Oh, then, dear lady, deem me not remiss
  In that I have but seldom set apart
Thy name in praiseful song. My singing is,
  Like any child's, a thing devoid of art;
But joy it hath and thine all praise for this—
  I sing beneath the shelter of thy heart.

Kiss Her

Say, young man! if you've a wife,
      Kiss her.
Every morning of your life,
      Kiss her.
Every evening when the sun
Marks your day of labor done,
Get you homeward on the run—
      Kiss her!

Even though you're feeling bad,
      Kiss her.
If she's out of sorts and sad,
      Kiss her.
Act as if you meant it, too;
Let the whole true heart of you
Speak its ardor when you do
      Kiss her.

If you think it's "soft," you're wrong.
      Kiss her.
Love like this will make you strong.
      Kiss her.
If you'd strike with telling force
At the Evil of Divorce,
Just adopt this simple course:
      Kiss her.

Dear Unselfish Dan

(A SOUTH JERSEY BALLAD)

Most everyone that knowed our Dan
Agreed he was the kindest man
They ever see. He had the knack
Of takin' on his own broad back
The burdens an' the slaps and pokes
Belonged by rights to other folks.
If anyone was in distress
An' went to Dan, he'd say: "I guess
We'll pull you out all right; let's see,
Suppose you leave all that to me."

Was nothin' finer than the way
He cared for poor old Uncle Jay,
Who was the most unlucky han'
For havin' trouble with his lan'
'Bout taxes, or the early spring
Plowin', or some other thing
That plumb upsot the poor old man.
Then, in the nick o' time, our Dan
Steps in, and sez, "Don't fret," sez he,
"Suppose you leave all that to me."

It got to be that Uncle Jay
He couldn't git along no way
Without our Dan, an' our Dan he
Jest cared fur him unselfishly.
An' when the old man come to die
Our Dan, o' course, was right close by.
Sez Uncle Jay: "I'm worrit, Dan,
'Bout what's to come of all my lan'

An' all my money out at loan,
An' in the bank, when I am gone."
Then Dan, he ups an' sez, sez he:
"Suppose you leave all that to me."

A Frosty Morning

I love these frosty mornings,
  When all the outer air
Is tingling with a freshness
  And vim beyond compare.

The north-wind in the tree-tops
  Proclaims the coming dawn,
And sends the crisp leaves rattling
  Across the frozen lawn.

From some adjacent farmyard
  A watchful chanticleer,
With raucous, joyous crowing
  Assails the atmosphere.

Then, nearer home, a watchdog,
  Awakened from his sleep,
Gives voice to his resentment
  In tones prolonged and deep.

A wagon, bound for market,
  Goes creaking down the road.
I hear the axles groaning
  Beneath the heavy load.

The light grows at my window,
  And on the pane, I see,
Jack Frost has limned a picture
  Of silvery tracery.

Now, from the servants' stairway,
  Slow feet descend the hall;

And then a kitchen shutter
　　Bangs out against the wall.

I love, these frosty mornings,
　　To note these things, and then—
To draw the bed-clothes closer,
　　And go to sleep again.

The Wisdom of the Sparrows

'Twas a city sparrow, wise and debonair,
  Idly loafing through the country with his mate.
Stupid country birds were building everywhere,
  For the nesting-time was growing very late,
    But the sparrow, with his lady,
    In a tree-top, cool and shady,
Gazed with scorn upon the work and twittered: "Stuff!"
    To his mate he chirruped shrilly:
    "Isn't all this labor silly,
When a roosting-place at night is quite enough?"

'Twas a motherly old robin, near at hand,
  Who was busy at her building with the rest,
And she turned upon the sparrows to demand
  How they meant to hatch their eggs without a nest.
    "Such impertinence!" half sadly
    Said the sparrow; "and yet gladly
I'll impart to you the knowledge that you beg."
    Then, with haughty condescension,
    He remarked: "I need but mention
That it's possible to obviate the egg."

'Twas a congress of the birds of every sort,
  All indignantly assembled to protest
Their displeasure, when the robin made report
  Of the threatened abolition of the nest;
    And they spoke of it as "awful!"
    "Selfish," "scandalous," "unlawful,"
And they prophesied "the country's speedy fall."
    But the sparrows, quite disdaining
    All this ignorant complaining,
Simply went their way, unmindful of it all.

'Twas a sage old owl, a very solemn bird,
  Sat and listened while his feathered fellows fought.
Never once he oped his mouth to say a word,
  But he did a lot of thinking—and he thought:
    "So the sparrows think it best
    To abolish eggs and nest.
Well, perhaps the wisdom isn't theirs at all,
    But a plan of good Dame Nature's
    To eliminate such creatures.
Let them have their way; the loss is mighty small."

To a Plain Sweetheart

I love thee, dear, for what thou art,
  Nor would I wish thee otherwise,
For when thy lashes lift apart
  I read, deep-mirrored in thine eyes,
The glory of a modest heart.

Wert thou as fair as thou art good,
  It were not given to any man,
With daring eyes of flesh and blood,
  To look thee in the face and scan
The splendor of thy womanhood.

Night in Bachelor's Hall

They've gone away! It seems a year,
Aye! weeks of years, since they were here;
And yet it was but yesterday
I kissed them when they went away,
Away from all the scorching heat
That grips this brick-walled city street.
And it was I who bade them go,
Though she, dear heart, protested so,
And vowed I'd find no joy at all,
Nor any peace, in Bachelor's Hall.
I laughed at that, but she was right;
I never knew a sadder night
Than this, while thus I tread, alone,
These silent halls I call my own.
I never thought this place could change
So utterly and seem so strange.
The night is hot, and yet a chill
Pervades the house; it is so still.
I miss the living atmosphere
That comforts me when they are here;
I miss the sigh, long-drawn and deep,
The music of refreshing sleep,
That undulates the gentle breast
Of weary motherhood at rest.
And in the unaccustomed gloom
That shrouds the small adjoining room
I miss the moans, the muffled screams,
Of childhood troubled in its dreams.
And is this all? No! more I miss
The strong, heart-thrilling joy, the bliss
Of warding, with protecting arm,
Between these precious hearts and harm.

O! sing your song, all ye who roam,
Your wistful song of "Home, Sweet Home,"
But, though unhappy is your lot,
You will not find a sadder spot
In all the world than Home, when they
Who make it Home have gone away.

To an Old Lover

There is silvery frost on your hair, old boy,
  There are lines on your forehead, too;
But your clear eyes speak of the peace and joy
  That dwell in the heart of you.
For the passing of youth you have no regret,
  No sighs for the summer gloam
And the lovers' moon. They are with you yet
  In the light of the lamp at home.

In your summer of youth, in that sunny hour
  That will come to you never again,
When you wooed your love as the bee the flower,
  The sweets that you gathered then
You have hived and stored for your later life,
  And your heart is the honeycomb—
Ah! I've seen your face when you kissed your wife
  In the light of the lamp at home.

O! you rare old lover! O! faithful knight,
  With your sweetheart of long ago.
You are many days from the warmth and light
  Of the summers you used to know;
But you need not yearn for the glamor and gold
  Of the fields you were wont to roam—
O! the light for the hearts that are growing old
  Is the light of the lamp at home.

Almost

"There stands the parson's house," he said.
The maiden hung her modest head,
Lest he who thus was moved to speak
Should note the blush that dyed her cheek.
The moonlit fields, the sky above,
Were mutely eloquent of love;
And love surcharged the ambient air
Breathed in by this young rustic pair.
With beating hearts, across the road,
They saw the minister's abode.
The study lamp a welcome gleamed,
And, through the summer twilight, seemed
Inviting them to near the door.
"There stands the parson's house!" Once more
His fervid thoughts broke forth in speech.
Then silence, thrilling each to each,
Surrounded them and held them mute.
Far-off they heard an owlet hoot
"To whit! to woo!" The maiden's heart
Was warm for him, but hers the part
In modesty to wait the word
That she in fancy oft had heard,
And which, instinctively she knew,
Was trembling on his tongue. He, too,
Was conscious of his own love's strength,
And meant to speak. He said, at length:
"There stands the parson's house, and there—"
His hand a-tremble cleft the air—
"Is where it used to stand!" And then
He led her down the road again.

The Little Boy

The little boy Jack was a Jack o' Hearts,
  For everyone loved the lad,
And the birds from near and foreign parts
  Were some of the friends he had.
The man in the Moon was his friend at night.
  When little Jack's prayers were said,
And his doting mother had dimmed the light
  And cuddled him up in bed,
He'd lie and talk to his friend in the skies
  Through the casement open wide,
And ask if the stars were not the eyes
  Of good little boys who had died.

O! the Moon-Man laughed at this odd conceit
  Of his little boy friend on earth,
And the wee stars, clustered about his feet,
  Just winked at his childish mirth.
But once when the moon rose over the hill
  And shone on the cottage wall,
The birds in the neighboring trees were still
  And a gloom hung over all.
Then the Moon-Man wondered much of Jack,
  And he pondered it o'er and o'er,
Till he saw two stars in the sky at his back
  That he never had seen before.

Rubicam Road

Where, in all the wide world, is the loveliest street?
There are millions of roads trod by billions of feet,
And the question, if asked of each traveler you meet,
  Will produce a reply of a different mode.
There are many in this unregenerate day
Who will speak for "Fifth Avenue," aye, or "Broadway,"
But the fortunate few who are wiser will say:
  "It is Rubicam Road!"

O! then sneer, if you will, and make game of our claim;
Aye! and have your rude fling at the old-fashioned name
And the rural aroma that clings to the same.
  Yet no beauty so rare ever glimmered and glowed
From the lamps of the tall-towered towns of the world,
Upon streets where humanity jostled and swirled,
As the beauty that's daily and nightly unfurled
  Over Rubicam Road.

Here's a street of the city, yet skirting a wood
Where the town's brazen clamors but seldom intrude;
"Rus in urbe," indeed with all graces imbued
  That old Horace himself might have shrined in an ode!
For the shadows are coolest, the sun is most bright,
The queen moon and the stars shed the kindliest light,
And the peace is the sweetest that droppeth at night
  Over Rubicam Road.

You will never believe it, and yet it is true!
I can prove it to you, sir—and you, sir—and you!
You have only to go there and do as I do.
  You have simply to go and take up your abode—

Be the latter as humble and plain as it may—
Where Her kiss in the morning that speeds you away
Will be drawing you back, at the close of the day,
  Into Rubicam Road.

All's Well

How fared the fight with thee today?
   Not well? Ah, nay,
Thou hast not lost; thou canst not lose,
However much they tear and bruise
The panting breast, the straining thews
 Which are thy spirit's citadel,
If thou and Faith, upon the walls,
Are comrades still when darkness falls.
  Rest now! In sleep thy veins shall swell
  With Hope's new wine; and like a bell
From valleys deep heard on the height,
Thy 'leaguered soul, throughout the night,
 Shall call to thee: "All's well!"

It is thyself alone that may
   Thyself betray.
Arise again! Arise and fight!
God's smile is in the morning light;
Lift thou thy banner brave and bright
 Above thy spirit's citadel!
What matter if its fall be sure?
The pilgrim soul thy walls immure,
 Clinging the wings of Azrael,
 In face of all the hordes of hell,
Shall take, full-armed, its homeward flight,
And o'er thy ruins, from the height,
 Shall call to thee: "All's well!"

The Birth o' Tam o' Shanter

[To a friendly challenge from Captain Grose we are indebted for this admirable masterpiece (Tam o' Shanter). Burns having entreated him to make honorable mention of Alloway Kirk in his Antiquities of Scotland, he promised compliance with the request upon condition that the poet should supply him with a metrical witch story as an accompaniment to the engraving. Mrs. Burns it was who related to Kromek the marvelous rapidity with which this poem was produced. According to her, it was the work of a single day, * * * as Alexander Smith puts it, with an exultant chuckle, the best day's work ever done in Scotland since Bruce won Bannockburn. Burns, during the early part of that memorable day, had passed the time alone in pacing his favorite walk, upon the river bank. Thither in the afternoon he was followed by his "bonnie Jean" and some of their children. Finding that he was "crooning to himself," and fearing lest their presence might be an interruption, his considerate wife loitered some little distance behind among the bloom and heather with her brood of young ones. There her attention was caught by the poet's impassioned gesticulations. She could hear him repeating aloud, while the tears ran down his face: "Now, Tam! O, Tam! had they been queans." Toward evening, when the storm of composition had fairly run out, Burns, we are told by M'Diarmid, committed the verses to writing upon the top of a sod dyke, overhanging the river; and directly they were completed rushed indoors to read them aloud by the fireside in a tone of rapturous exultation.]—Rev. Dr. J. Loughran Scott, in the Alloway Edition of Burns' Works.

[Read before the Burns Club of St. Louis on January 25, 1916.]

How broke the east upon that day,
In fire and blood or ashes gray?
And did a rich or niggard boon
Of sunlight gild the Nith at noon?
Who knows or cares? For on that morning,
When Tam o' Shanter, without warning,
Came gloriously down to earth,
The river, singing at his birth,
Wore on its face a mystic light;
For in that moment reached its height

The lyric fire, the dying flare
From out the heart of Burns of Ayr!

O! little Nith! O! happy river,
You shall not lose that gleam forever;
Your waves, whatever moods betide them,
Shall sing of him who walked beside them
And from his great heart wove a story
That was the crown upon his glory.
And on that morning when he came
With frenzied eye and cheek aflame
To feast his soul upon the food
That poets find in solitude,
What was the charm you held him with,
O! helpful little river Nith?
Ah, well I know the way you did it!
I shall not mince nor gloss the credit,
But, auditing the dim dead past,
Shall here set down your score at last.

To you, that morning (Who shall care
If skies above were dull or fair?)
The poet, seeking comfort, brought
His fecund fancy, big with thought.
Beside your bonnie banks he walked,
And ever as he went he talked
The quaint, blithe things that thronged his brain
And conned them o'er and o'er again;
And presently the liquid laughter
Of pleasant waters gurgled after,
And, as a voice by harp attended,
With borrowed beauty grows more splendid,
So waxed the poet's budding song
Where light your ripples leaped along.

You smiled and danced and made your measures
To match his song of ale-house pleasures,
Where Tam and cronies came to mingle
Beside their comfortable ingle;
But when the "reaming swats" came thicker
And Robin's tongue, that sang of liquor,
Grew overloud and full of yearning,
No doubt you set your rapids churning,
To draw his thoughts from off the "nappy"
And keep him singing, blithe and happy.
Then, when he pushed those joys aside
And sallied forth with Tam to ride,
(For well you know that Tam o' Shanter
Was not alone upon that canter)
How well again his mood was fellowed!
Among your rocks the thunder bellowed;
Your spray upon the light breeze passed
For "rattlin' showers upon the blast";
You made the "Doon pour all his floods,"
The "doubling storm roar through the woods";
And somewhere in your shadows lurk
The dancers in the ruined kirk.

But when that dance grew wild and furious
And Tam, with watching, much too curious;
And Robin, prattling of the "queans,
A' plump and strapping in their teens,"
Seemed bent on lingering overlong,
I like to think that then the song
In all your rippling waves you stilled,
As by the breath of winter chilled,
That Robin, in the pause, might hear
His "bonnie Jean" and children near;

And draw his thoughts from "sarks o' flannel"
And back into the proper channel.

.   .   .   .   .   .

Then with your song and liquid laughter
You rose again to follow after,
With O! what sympathetic feeling,
Where faithful Meg, the mare, goes reeling
Across the bridge that spans the flood,
By all the ghostly crew pursued,
And carries off her master, hale,
But leaves behind her own grey tail.

And when the day was done you knew
The poet's exaltation, too;
'Twas yours at fall of dusk to share
The calm that soothed the Bard of Ayr,
And through the night, O happy stream!
You were a music in his dream.
There, musing by some mossy stone,
Perhaps, ah, yes, you must have known
That though again upon your shore
The poet still would walk, no more
Would Time bring round to you the bliss
Of any day to match with this—
The very cap-sheaf on the past,
The greatest labor and the last.
Oh! in the fire of that one day
How many years were burned away?
And in the torrents of his tears
Were lost how many unborn years?
For this man took life's cup and laughed
And strove to drain it at a draught,
What tragedy was in this mirth,
O! river, singing at its birth?

What holocaust was in the light
With which your morning face was bright?

O! little Nith! O! happy river,
You shall not lose that gleam forever;
Your waves, whatever moods betide them,
Shall sing of him who walked beside them
And from his great heart wove a story
That was the crown upon his glory!

Summer's Swan-song

O! have ye seen Rogue Autumn?
  He's hiding hereabout
To rob me of my green domain
  And put my birds to rout.
He's marshaling his army;
  The skirmishers are out.
"All's well! All's well!" the katydids,
  His nightly pickets, shout.

Rogue Autumn, bold pretender,
  Conspiring with the sun,
Is working in the morning mists
  That I may be undone.
Already through my fields and woods
  The fires of treason run;
My myriad leaves are putting on
  His colors, one by one.

Thy breath at night, Rogue Autumn,
  Strikes chill upon my brow;
My crown uneasy rests upon
  The head I soon must bow.
Take thou thy spoil! But there will come
  A mightier than thou,
Whose winds shall pierce and break thy heart,
  As mine is breaking now!

"Ada Rehan Is Dead"

Those few lines on the printed page
Call up for me a darkened stage. . . .
And Fancy in the shadowy wings
Paints ghosts of dear, once happy things—
Bright elves which in that place had birth
Of clear-eyed Truth and frolic Mirth,
And, having filled their hour of grace,
Now, mute, on tiptoe, haunt the place. . . .
Nor light nor any sound is there
To strike across the brooding air,
But still a sense above it all
Of something evil to befall. . . .
Then sounds, off-stage, one tap—no more—
As of a knuckle on a door,
And with the sound a gust upblows,
Chill as the breath of Arctic snows;
The grisly call-boy in the dark
Is waiting at the threshold. Hark!
He speaks! His tones sepulchral frame
The loved, but half-forgotten, name.
A brave, sweet voice makes answering hail,
And merging with it breaks a wail
Of sobbing in the upper air. . . .
A thin light stabs the dark—and there
A youth—nay, but the merest boy—
Who loved this Priestess of Pure Joy,
Leans from the gallery and peers
Down, stageward, through a mist of tears. . . .
The weeping stops; the last faint note
Chokes back into my aching throat,
For in this boyish mourner see
The lad that once I used to be. . . .

With all a boy's abandonment
I loved her then, this Heaven-sent
Interpreter of all the moods
And womanly beatitudes.
I loved her graceful ways and each
Delicious little trick of speech
That marked her dearer than the rest,
But O! my heart was happiest
In this, which in that heart I knew:
That she was wholly sweet and true. . . .
I mourn for her, but are these tears
Not also for the buried years?
And for the thought that with her dies
Another of the crumbling ties
Between me and my happy youth?
Ah, yes, I know it, and the truth
Makes sudden riot in the heart,
Where once she queened it with her art.

A Summer Idyll

The scene: A public city square,
With crowded benches here and there.
The time: A drowsy afternoon,
Charged with the heady wine of June.
Chief actors: Voice, Law's voice, supreme
And harsh with petty power: and Dream,
A vagrant sprite that stops to play
'Round one old head unkempt and gray.

THE DREAM:

Ah! rest. How far off seems the street—
Its heat still tingles in my feet,
But Lord! how sweet this is, how sweet!—
And O! the shade, this blessed shade
That all the little leaves have made—
The little leaves—they're whispering now—
Whispering? They're singing on the bough!
How clear and sweet the whole tree sings—
Tree? It's a golden bird with wings!
How soft its back is! Sweet to lie
Snug in its feathers here and fly
Where Heaven is so wide and clear—

THE VOICE:

Hey! Set up straight; ye can't sleep here!

THE DREAM:

. . . The nurse-maid smiled,
But she looked kind; so did the child.

205

What dimpled cheeks! so round, so fair,
Like peaches. . . . Peaches, everywhere!
Wait, little boy, don't climb the trees.
See how the fruit swings in the breeze.
Lie here with me until they fall.
Here where the grass is thick and tall,
Stretch yourself out and lie at ease.
Don't shake! don't shake! don't shake the trees!
Here they come pelting down like rain—

THE VOICE:

Here, Bo! I warn ye onct again.

THE DREAM:

. . . His coat is blue,
Yet Heaven has the self-same hue;
How odd; . . . His belt looks tight in back,
And mine—it never was so slack.
Somewhere, somewhere, there's bread and meat;
Somewhere, perhaps, but then the street—
If I could wet my face and hair
With water from that fountain there—
How sparklingly the ripples break,
And what a pleasant sound they make!
Drip! drip! . . . the mill-wheel turns so slow,
So slow, so slow— Ah! there's a fish!
He's in the net! Now for a dish
That any royal king might wish! . . .
O! peaceful pipe beside the fire—
The moon's up now and rising higher.
Snug is the camp, crisp-cool the night,
The embers flare up, warm and bright!

The waves of heat that beat, beat, beat,
Upon the weary, way-worn feet—

THE VOICE:

I warned you twice an' now you're done,
Git out o' here! Move on! move on!

The Song of the March Wind

I am the minstrel, the maker of mirth,
  And the forest my harp is:
From the fibres asleep in the heart of the earth,
  Where its woof and its warp is,
      I fashion the spring
      With the song that I sing!

I, that am breathed of the mouth of my God,
  Am His music in motion;
And His breath on my winds shakes the slumbering sod
  And the floor of the ocean;
      And I fashion the spring
      With the song that I sing!

I am the breath of your nostrils, O man!
  And akin to your spirit;
But our God's voice was mine ere your singing began,
  So rejoice when you hear it;
      For I bring you the spring
      With the song that I sing!

Miss Maple o' Norway

Miss Maple o' Norway,
   So slender, so dear,
She has brightened our doorway
   This many a year,
For the beauty adorning her, morning and night,
Is our darling delight.

What a maidenly thing
She appeared in the spring,
Where demurely she stood
In her virginal snood;
And the staid greens become her
Through all the long summer,
But autumn, the mummer,
Comes galloping in—
And her troubles begin!
For the wastrel October,
Who never is sober,
Was quick to enrobe her
In raiment of gold,
And the maiden grew bold—
Ah! the tale is soon told . . .
She was looking her best
In the blaze from the west,
When the sun sank to rest
Where the wild storm was brewing
That wrought her undoing . . .
Two rivals came wooing—
Two rogues of a kind,
The Rain and the Wind—
And the maid, nothing loath,
Gallivanted with both . . .

All the night long I heard her
Fox-trotting with Murder,
In that death-dance insane—
With the Wind and the Rain!
And the gray morning found her—
Poor "Lady of Pain"—
With all her gold glory strewn tatters around her.

Miss Maple o' Norway,
　This desolate morn,
Still stands at our doorway,
　But cold and forlorn.
Poor little, deluded, denuded young thing!
Let her sleep until spring!

The Mother

She was so frail, my little one,
  She had not yet begun to stir
Her tiny limbs; from sun to sun,
  This breast, these arms maternal were
  The bounded universe for her.

But now far spaces feel her might,
  And sad, sweet thoughts of her arise
With every sun; she stirs the night
  With sighing winds, and from the skies
  She looks at me with starry eyes.

To a Little Girl of Five

I wish your eyes might always look
  As big with love as now they seem.
It cannot be! Your picture-book,
Whose leaves we turned together, took
  Away my dream.

It was the old man on that page
  Who bore the hour-glass and scythe.
That rude reminder of old age!
With what a rush of inward rage
  He made me writhe!

He stirred you, too, to frown and say:
  "The ugly thing! And who is he?"
"That man, my dear," I said, "some day
Is going to come and steal away
  Your heart from me."

"Oh, no!" you said. But it is true;
  Unless in some way we contrive
To fill that old man's path with glue
And keep me forty-eight, and you
  Forever five!

Inscription for a Fireplace

I'm Home's heart! Warmth I give and light,
   If you but feed me.
I blossom in the winter night,
   When most you need me.

To melt your cares, to warm your guest,
   My cheer's supplied you;
But, O! to know me at my best,
   Hold Her beside you!

Romany Rye *

Romany rye, all the world's in high feather now—
    Earth, sea and sky.
Romany roads, in this midsummer weather now
    Goldenly lie.
Take which you will of them, this one that sallies
Up through the piney hills, that for the valleys,
Dunes by the salt marsh, or leafy green alleys,
    Bearing no pack but the lilt of a song with you.
Aye! but a love-lilt another may share
Makes the best road-song for banishing care;
She who is mate to you, still young and fair,
    Take Her along with you,
      Romany rye!

Romany rye, what to you are the gypsy folk,
    Sordid and sly?
You and your Queen shall be wisest of tipsy folk,
    Drunk with the sky,
Drunk with the wine of this midsummer weather,
Drunk with your wedded hearts toiling together—
Brawlers as sinless as bees in the heather,
    Bearing home all the day's sweets at the end of it.
Aye! for what Romany road you may roam
Still shall it circle, through sunset and gloam,
Drawing you surely and happily home
    Round the last bend of it,
      Romany rye!

* Gypsy gentleman.

Grace for the Ship

In the days, before steam, when the brigs and the clippers
   Were the beautiful queens of the world's seven seas,
We were second to none in the breed of our skippers,
   For Liberty's self was the mother of these,
They were masterful, hardy, rough, ready and keen.
As befitted the Lords of the Merchant Marine—
   But when seas were to conquer and wild men to tame,
Not another "old man" of the clipper-ship days
Matched the smiling Len Barrett, who fashioned the phrase:
   "Eat hearty, and give the old ship a good name!"

Oh, full many a ship was a despot's dominion,
   When a waste of wide water washed 'round the oak throne,
And a marlin-spike scepter discouraged opinion—
   But Cap'n Len Barrett had ways of his own.
'Twas with lightning and laughter, a double-edged smile,
That he flogged down the sea-lawyers spreading their guile;
   And the budding disloyalty died, when he came,
With a lip of wreathed sunshine and eye of cold steel,
To propose as a grace for the fo'castle meal:
   "Eat hearty, and give the old ship a good name!"

Here's a leaf from the past for all needs of the present;
   Here's a grace for our Ship of State, Captain and crew.
Is the vessel not stately? The voyage not pleasant?
   Then where does the trouble lie? Mayhap in you.
There are sea-lawyers now as in wind-jamming days,
And the good ship *America,* mete for all praise,
   Cannot wholly be rid of these birds of ill fame;
But here's grace for the rest of us happy to share
In the burdens, the triumphs, the bountiful fare:
   "Eat hearty, and give the old ship a good name!"

Hymn to the Sun

Whistles of noon!
And soon
Echoing alley and street
Sound to the myriad feet
That shuffle or loiter or run.
Hark to your worshipers there,
Baring their souls to the air;
Hark to them making their prayer,
Hear them, O Sun!

Out of the white
Cold light
Flooding the counters of trade
Issues the mid-day parade.
Glad of these moments of play
Snatched from the heart of the day,
How many toilers renew
Joy o' life, worshiping you,
Builder, whose dream-castles rear
Here in these wastes of the year.
Stirred by your promise of spring,
Fancy, a bird on the wing,
Soars over many a creek
Where the brown trout are to seek,
Soars over links, over field
Where there are pleasures to yield,
And for which longed-for delight
Hosts pray increase of your might.
Others there be who but live
Here in this hour that you give;
Clerks and the keepers of books
Praise you, O Sun, with their looks,

Praise you with throbbings that start
Voiceless but strong, in the heart.
Eyes that observe how the snow
Drips from the eaves, in your glow,
And how the pools in the street
Smile back at Heaven, repeat
Mute but deep homage no less.
Even your lightest caress,
Even your smokiest ray,
Haltingly finding its way
Into some corner of gloom,
Shut in a mouldering room,
Stirreth some spirit to grope
Back to the borders of hope.

    Planet of Noon!
    Come soon
Into the haunts of the poor.
Pain too sharp to endure
Into their days hath run.
    They whom the fates still hold
    Thralls of the hunger and cold
    Beg for your healing gold.
Hear them, O Sun!

On the Road to Arden

As I went down by Granther's Glade
   Upon the road to Arden,
I stopped to rest me in the shade
   Beside a sunny garden.
So sultry burned the afternoon
The very heavens seemed to swoon;
So still lay all the countryside
That little sounds were magnified.
Behind me, in the hollyhocks,
The bees were loud as chiming clocks!
   I heard them boom:
   "Zoom! zoom! zoom! zoom!"
And long I marveled in the shade
   Beside that sunny garden,
As I went down by Granther's Glade
   Upon the road to Arden.

Upon the little bridge that spanned
   The mill-stream's tinkling water,
I passed the miller's 'prentice and
   The miller's budding daughter.
Her bell-shaped bonnet hid her face;
They stood, removed a little space,
And listless leaned above the weir.
So still! I fancied I could hear—
What else but those same booming clocks,
The loud bees in the hollyhocks?
   A pulselike beat:
   "Sweet! sweet! sweet! sweet!"
Yet listless stood the 'prentice and
   The miller's budding daughter,

Upon the little bridge that spanned
  The mill-stream's tinkling water.

"To find a bonnet, like a bell,
  With a rose face thereunder,
Might fool a bee that loved too well
  His share of sugared plunder."
Thus musing, slow I climbed the hill—
Then, sudden, on the air so still
There burst so sure a booming sound,
I stopped, and quickly turned me round.
A low branch hid the bridge from sight,
And yet—so near! I must be right—
  "Zoom! sweet! zoom! sweet!"
  The notes repeat.
"Some bee," I said, "that loves too well
  His share of sugared plunder,
Has found a bonnet like a bell
  With a rose face thereunder."

Here's Company

If kindred wood but lend its grace
    And, burning free,
Make sunlight from this chimney-place
    To shine on me;
And one alone come here to rest,
    What need have we
For other guest? The place is blest—
    Here's company!

Forlorn and lonely? No one here
    Can ever be!
Here is fraternity of cheer;
    Are we not three,
The chimney-nook and I and thou?
    At least, agree
Sad looks but ill become thee now—
    Here's company!

Yet, man, my arms—once leafy boughs
    Upon a tree—
Are, oh, so fitly formed to house
    Thy mate and thee.
On snowy nights, when here, heart-bound,
    Nest thou and She,
May no disturbing doorbell sound:
    "Here's company!"

Foch!

Out of the grandeur and peace
Of the high Pyrenees,
That nested and nurtured him, came
He, the young eaglet predestined for fame.
Quietly brooding, maturing his wings and his power,
He bided his hour.
It came; and he rose in his might,
Armed doubly with Valor and Right,
And under the sweep of his wings
Saw topple the thrones of vain Kings;
Nor rested, till out of the flame
And horror the Victory came,—
And the shining star of his name!
But over all, Peace to the World.

. . . .

Now let the banners be furled,
And the tumult of voices be dumb!
The hour, the hour has come!
Strong-winged, through the ultimate night,
Once more to his home on the height—
The glory and peace of the height—
The Eagle has taken his flight!

March 20, 1929

Aged Bard, to Himself

So, here's the year, the month, the day!
And, on this twenty-eighth of May,
The sixtieth milestone on your way,
What message of affection, pray,
Could I—could anyone—convey
    To you, you old curmudgeon?
Now, wait! Tut! tut! for goodness' sake!
Don't strain your arteries to break
    The record for the old high dudgeon!

Why should you look for words of praise
Or any sort of gay bouquets
Because, forsooth, another year
Still finds you idly loitering here?
And why should people cry: "Hail! hail!"
To you, poor fish? You're not a whale,
    But just the smallest sort of gudgeon.
Don't fuss so much about your birthdays.
You've had your share, and more, of mirth-days,
And now you're in your ample-girth days;
    And if kind Death withholds his bludgeon
And lets you reach, say, sixty-five,
Well, just be glad that you're alive!

Memorial Day, 1931

God's Acre smiles beneath this sky of May.
 And yet, behold! between us and the sun,
This moment when with reverent hands we lay
 Our wreaths on heroes' graves, grim shadows run—
In serried flight, wings flash and motors roar;
The fleets of air are prophesying war!

So, must there be increase
 Of graves to strew with rue and immortelle,
 Ere we inherit these who fought and fell
That we might live in peace?

"Let us have peace!" How long ago we raised
 Above the desolation of fair fields,
Above the ruined homes where Sorrow gazed
 In dark despair at Hate's unholy yields,
That fervent aspiration to have done
With man-made clouds that veil the genial sun.

"Henceforth all war must cease,"
 We told each other, with approving nods,
 "The heart of man shall beat in tune with God's;
Let us have peace!"

"Let us have peace!" How long ago we found
 An ugly quaver jangling in the note;
Above the chorus clashed the steely sound
 Of swords still naked at a brother's throat,
And down the wind, from shipyard, shop and mill,
Came murmurs of new readiness to kill.

War's fathered by alarm;
   "Let us have peace!" is not enough to say.
   The sword is sheathed; it must be laid away.
Let us disarm!

The Cold Spell

The other mornin' early, when the cold began to bite
  An' I heerd the rafters crackin' an' my breath wuz full o'
    smoke,
An' the first faint spark o' daylight showed the winders frosted
    white,
  I remarked to Ann Eliza thet some records would be broke.
Then a wagon on the turnpike crunched the brittle snow like
    glass,
  An' I heerd the harness snappin' an' the horses snortin' there—
But I didn't git a notion what a freeze had come to pass
  Till I seen ole Peleg Tuttle settin' speechless in his chair.

Thar wuz signs aroun' the barnyard when I went to do my chores
  Thet wuz eloquent thet somethin' out o' common had occurred,
Fur the dash-dinged Ar'tic Circle seemed a-campin' right out-
    doors;
  An' the very air wuz frozen, fur it never even stirred.
But I didn't sense the bigness o' the freeze thet had arrove
  Till I drove up to the village store, behind my old gray mare,
An' I hollered out "Good mornin'!" to the boys aroun' the stove—
  An' I see ole Peleg Tuttle settin' speechless in his chair.

Oh, they tell us thet a freeze-up is no blessin', but a curse;
  But I vum if it's a good one it may still be somethin' more,
Fur your little half-baked freezes are a mighty darn-site worse
  Since they loosen up the chatter o' the oldest village bore.
Now the one thet we been havin' is a harder freeze than those
  Thet ever struck this neighborhood fur mebbe fifty year,
Fur, by heck! his reminiscences wuz absolutely froze
  When I see old Peleg Tuttle settin' speechless in his chair.

Song of the Christmas Tree

Once out of midnight sweet with mystery
The wonder of all wonders came to be;
So shall the dawn a marvel make of me.
For when in all my beauty I am born
In the first glimmer of the Christmas morn,
Angels of innocence in mortal guise
Shall look upon me with their faith-big eyes;
      And, looking, see
      A greater thing in me
Than the bare figure of a tree.
      Behold! in every limb
      I thrill with praise of Him
For whom I stand in memory.

Kings of the East and wise men three there were
Who brought to Him rare frankincense and myrrh.
So do my balsamed branches when they stir
In the warm airs that move about this room,
And render forth their homage in perfume.
Lift up your hearts anew, O! care-worn men,
Look up with glad, believing eyes again;
      And, looking, see
      A greater thing in me
Than the bare figure of a tree.
      Behold! in every limb
      I thrill with praise of Him
For whom I stand in memory.

The Man's Prayer

When all is still within these walls,
And Thy sweet sleep through darkness falls
On little hearts that trust in me,
However bitter toil may be,
For length of days, O Lord! on Thee,
        My spirit calls.

Their daily need by day enthralls
My hand and brain, but when night falls
And leaves the questioning spirit free
To brood upon the days to be,
For time and strength, O Lord! on Thee
        My spirit calls.

The April Fool

Here's April come to her own again,
    And her own, as wild as she,
Rise up when her green flag's flown again
    On sod and bush and tree.
Oh, "there's no fool like an old fool"
    (As the wise men all agree),
And I doubt if there comes
To follow her drums
    Another to match with me.

The bulk of my days are the formal ones,
    Untroubled of trifling dreams,
And the thoughts they breed are the normal ones
    Of envy, worry and schemes.
But, "there's no fool like an old fool,"
    And a glint of April sky,
Or a bird in the rain,
Will twist my brain,
    And the fool of the world am I!

In winter's cold there is pain enough
    In meeting the debts I owe;
I pity myself and am sane enough
    To envy the rich I know.
But, "there's no fool like an old fool,"
    And the gold of an April day,
While I gather my share,
Will make me swear
    I am rich in a nobler way.

Yet they will say, with their sneers for me,
    That mine is a sorry life,

Since the total yield of the years for me
    Is a roof and a rose-gray wife;
For there's no fool like the poor fool
    Who hasn't the wit to see
How the glory that stirs
My heart and hers
    Makes a king of the world of me.

Virtuous Blank Verse

Even the names of the alcoholic beverages should be banished from our literature.

—*Prohibition Circular*.

Begin with Dickens! Oh, my dear,
   His pen was much too handy
In praise of mugs of bitter ——,
   And tumblerfuls of ——.

And Robbie Burns! We must curtail
   His lines that grow too frisky
With talk of "reaming swats" of ——
   And goblets "fu'" of ——.

No tale in praise of any inn,
   Of cellar, vault or garret,
May say a word of Holland ——,
   Or even table ——.

Our writers now shall all be dumb
   On things that once were merry;
No talk shall be of steaming ——,
   Or glass of golden ——.

   .   .   .   .   .

No heights, no depths, beneath our sky,
   But all one perfect level;
Our country shall be hot and dry
   And saintly as the ——.

This Time o' Year

Just about this time o' year,
  On the heel of March, or later,
Some fine morning will appear
  God's own Labor Agitator.
    She (no daughter of a Viking,
    But a sweet maid to your liking),
Will, upon her bugle clear,
    Sound the signal to be striking,
Which you cannot choose but hear,
Just about this time o' year.

Just about this time o' year,
  Bursting through some rosy morning,
In the porches of your ear
  She will clamor without warning.
    She will bid you to be shirking
    Every sort of humdrum working.
Heed her! Follow! Have no fear!
    Wisdom, health and joy are lurking
In that gypsy call of cheer,
Just about this time o' year.

Just about this time o' year
  Let sweet Springtime ease your labor.
When she bids you "Strike!" give ear.
  Walk the fields, with her for neighbor.
    One wild day beside her dancing,
    Let her set your heart romancing,
And, with blood refreshed and clear,
    Send you back to labor, prancing!
Hark! Be ready! She is near
Just about this time o' year.

November

June is sweet, for then I found thee;
  But November, gray and cold,
Weaves warm memories around thee,
  Spun of gold.

June a rose-time we remember,
  Ere the boy became the man;
But in earnest with November
  Life began.

Still I see thee, as we threaded
  Gray woods under grayer skies;
Strange new hopes and fears were wedded
  In thine eyes.

And when these had been translated
  Into awed and reverent speech,
Stronglier then our souls were mated
  Each with each.

Deep with vernal promise laden,
  As with buds the leafless wood,
Here was blossoming of the maiden—
  Womanhood.

Rich the memories now that hover
  'Round that day when Life began,
And the lightheart boy, thy lover,
  Was a man.

To the Inconstant

Ye are the dullards, and not I,
  Ye conscienceless philanderers!
From one love to the next ye fly
  And are forever wanderers.
O! poor, blind votaries of the chase,
  Ye deem me coldly dutiful
Who, steadfast, watch one love-lit face
  Grow year by year more beautiful!

Each new love lives in your desire
  For but a moment's cherishing;
Your passion is a smouldering fire
  That is forever perishing,
That, seeking change, hath only found
  The ashes of satiety—
While mine hath but begun to sound
  Its one love's sweet variety!

The Living-room

Here throbs the home's deep heart!
From these four walls the full, warm spirits start,
Pulse through the halls, return, and richest bloom
In this small room.
For all who gather here when day is done,
But, most of all, for her, the central One,
  Whose great love to the whole doth warmth impart,
As to the lesser planets doth the Sun,
  Here throbs the home's deep heart.

This is a Queen's domain,
And all her subjects, happy in her reign,
Pray God she may, with her sweet woman's grace,
Long bless this place.
This is her court. The little airs that stir
About the room are eloquent of her.
  Each senseless thing whereon her hand hath lain
Becomes in its own way a courtier.
  This is a Queen's domain!

This is a holy spot.
Ah! pity for the man who knows it not!
But peace and holy calm, the light o' love
Knows nothing of,
The Queen's mate hath, when in the quiet night
He broods alone beside his ingle's light.
  He knows, when all his heart burns pure and hot
With thoughts too sweet to speak aloud or write,
  This is a holy spot!

The Queen's Fleets

Take for thy throne, my queen, this niche my hand
  Hath carved for thee,
Here in the gray breast of this dune of sand
  That fronts the sea.
In sovereign state aloof, the solitude
Hedging thee round, as once thy maidenhood,
Make me no partner of thy thought or speech
  This hour when day and darkness meet,
But count me merely jetsam of the beach,
  Here at thy feet.

It is mute beauty's hour. No late bird sings;
  Voiceless, serene,
The sea dreams; Silence holds all lovely things—
  And thou art queen!
For Silence, in the twilight's gold and red
Behind thee, sets a crown upon thy head.
Send forth, O Queen, thy fleets upon the main,
  Send forth thy daring fleets of thought,
And let me wait to hail them home again
  With riches fraught.

By Fancy captained, send thy fleets afar
  To win the sea;
Send them to know what spoils in ocean are,
  What mystery,
What beauty in all things that "suffered change"
In coral caves to "something rich and strange."
Then bring them home and I with kingly might
  Will take their treasure, as it lies
Safe-harbored in the starlit, purple night
  Of thy dear eyes.

235

Memory

Apple-blossoms, drenched with rain!
  Touched by the sun, how jewel-bright,
  Out of the night, the wild wet night,
They glimmer into my life again!
  And the sight
  Warms my heart with a young delight—
Stabs my soul with an old, old pain.

So was the picture framed, just so,
Once on a May-morn long ago . . .
Under the blossoming bough that day—
She was a blossom sweet as they—
My true love beckoned, smiled and said:
"Bestir yourself, O Sleepyhead!
Come, stand beside me here and see
How well the morning lights this tree . . .
There! lift your eyes, my dear, and look!"
Her quick hand caught the bough and shook
Its crystal freight upon my head.
She laughed her silver laugh and said:
"Poor dear! your eyes, your hair, your ears—
Your silly ears—are full of tears!
Bad girl! to tease the best of men—"
The minx was in my arms, and then
We kissed, beneath that fragrant bough . . .
All this was years ago, and now—

Apple-blossoms, drenched with rain!
  Touched by the sun, how jewel-bright,
  Out of the night—an age-long night—
They glimmer into my life again!
  And the sight
  Brings but tears for a lost delight—
Stabs my soul with an old, old pain.

Lovers' Quarrel

"The trouble with you,"
  The young man said,
As his eyes flashed blue
  And his face flushed red,
"Is lack of a few
  Ideas in your head!
    In fact,
    You act
  In a frivolous way;
    If you loved me true,
    As you say you do,
You'd pay some attention to what I say;
But so little attention to me you're paying
You never seem to know what I am saying."

"The trouble with you,"
  The Dear Thing said,
As she paused to renew
  Her lips' bright red,
"Is that you're too
  Much ruled by your head.
    In fact,
    You act
  Like a heartless crook!
    If you loved me true,
    As you say you do,
You'd pay some attention to how I *look;*
If the proper attention to me you were paying
You wouldn't know *yourself* what you were saying."

Mike Airedaly

(Nov., 1920–Nov., 1933)

We wonder, now that you have gone,
  That we should feel so little sorrow;
We seem to see you trudging on
  Through some unending glad Tomorrow,
Your stubby tail, your ears cocked up,
As gay as when you were a pup.

That's it! You were not happy here,
  Despite your patience in your blindness,
And we who loved you, Mike, old dear,
  Were acting with mistaken kindness;
We should have known, as now we know,
'Twere kinder to have let you go.

So, when your gentle doomsman led
  Your lagging feet beyond our portal,
We could not picture you as dead,
  But rather as a dear immortal!
For Death's quick stab, in very truth,
Restored you to eternal youth.

This house, which was your constant care—
  Was ever guardian more undaunted?—
So long as we are gathered there,
  Shall by your darling ghost be haunted,
And 'round the hearth-stone shall be sung
Your deeds when you were brave and young. . . .

Your collar, Mike, your leash and chain
  Still hang beside the kitchen dresser;

No doubt they'll come in use again
　　When we've selected your successor—
We'll seek, for night-watch gentleman,
Another of your Gaelic clan.

But, oh, my dear! you need not fear
　　That he will ever quite usurp you;
Your memory shall be deathless here,
　　You precious, pert, pugnacious purp, you!
And *his* best praise will be: "How like
This new lad is to dear old Mike!"

Solace

When you jeered at me, saying "Forget me,"
I feared that my heart wouldn't let me—
   But I find that the thing can be done,
   In the woods with a dog and a gun.

There's nepenthe and marvelous manna
For me—devotee of Diana—
   Flouting care as I joyously jog
   In the woods with a gun and a dog.

So, Proud Beauty, it's little I'm caring
How the world wags, so long as I'm faring—
   Where the thought of you never intrudes—
   With a gun and a dog in the woods.

Perennial May

May walks the earth again,
This old earth, and the same
Green spurts of tender flame
  Burn now on sod and tree
That burned when first she came,
  Dear love, to you and me.
  If any change there be—
    A great or a less
    Degree of loveliness—
  It is not ours to see,
        Dear love,
Not ours to feel or see.

May thrills our hearts again,
These old hearts, and the bough
Burns not with blossoms now
  That blow more splendidly.
For, since our wedded vow
  Made one of you and me,
  If any change there be—
    A greater or a less
    Degree of tenderness—
  It is not ours to see,
        Dear love,
Not ours to feel or see.

The Sanctum

Lord, God of love, the wedded heart's
   Sure Comforter,
O! make mine pure in all its parts,
   For Thee and Her!
Pour, Lord, the flood-tide of Thy grace
Through all its chambers, and efface
Each secret thought's abiding place.
   I pray thee make
One shrine of it, which Thou and she
May jointly share, that it may be
Open to her, Lord, as to Thee,
   For her dear sake.

Lord, God of love, who givest me
   Her heart of fire,
Long keep it mine, but let it be
   Not mine entire.
Though mine the honeyed tenderness,
That wells therein to cheer and bless
When joys elate or cares depress,
   I pray Thee make
Thy secret shrine within its core.
Let me before one close-sealed door
Cry "Non sum dignus" o'er and o'er
   For her dear sake.

Inspiration

"Good night," and then your candle's feeble flare
Went glimmering up the stair;
   A door closed and the house was still.
Slow hour by hour the night grew old,
And from the smouldering hearth the cold
   Stole forth and laid its chill
On fingers weary of the pen,
On heart and brain that had been fain
   To make a song of cheer.
For, oh, the summer warm and bright
You conjured in the winter night
Went upward with your candlelight,
   Went with you up the stair.

A Song for August

Here's the year on the wane.
  There are signs in the sky,
In the woods, on the plain,
  That its noon has gone by.
But the harvest's to gain
  And the cool nights are nigh,
When the year's on the wane.

Here's the year on the wane.
  There's a hawk in the blue;
In the wheat a red stain
  Where the poppy peeps through.
But there's bread in the grain
  And there's warmth o' love, too,
When the year's on the wane.

Here's the year on the wane.
  From the night-shrouded hill,
Comes the katydid's strain,
  And the wind's whistle shrill.
But two hearts may contain
  All the spring's music still,
When the year's on the wane.

The Christmas Reading

The herald winds of Christmas sleep
High-cradled on the wooded steep.
The far stars only are a-thrill
With life; the night is cold and still.
Come, gather 'round the ingle-nook
And from its shelf take down the book
Wherein the master's genius drew
Those pictures old, but ever new;
Whose "Christmas Carol's" deathless chime
Beats down the envious touch of time.
Here let the children sit, and there
Beneath the lamp's light place your chair.
Take up the book, O! golden voice,
And read the pages of your choice.
Tell us of Scrooge and Marley's ghost,
Of all our favorites old; but most,
Tell us with tenderness of him
We laugh and weep with—Tiny Tim.
Call up the soul to every face
About you in this holy place.
We shall not be ashamed at all
For frank, sweet tears you cause to fall;
But fervently, with eyelids dim
And hearts attuned to Tiny Tim,
We'll quote his words when you have done,
And say, "God bless us, every one!"

Darby and Joan

They come into the parlor car
　　And take their seats beside me.
How very commonplace they are!
　　I know my wife would chide me,
And call it rude of me to stare
　　At this old man and woman,
But, since they do not seem to care,
　　Why shouldn't I be human?
I've read my paper through and through—
　　There's mighty little in it—
And so I've nothing else to do
　　But watch them for a minute.
They offer little promise, though,
　　Of charm to the beholder;
I judge her sixty-five or so,
　　And he a trifle older. . . .

I've watched them for a hundred miles!
　　I'd watch another hundred,
To share the paradise that smiles
　　Around them! How I blundered,
To call this couple commonplace.
　　Youth's glory and Romance's
Play sunnily about each face
　　And glimmer in their glances.
His heart, a bee above the flower,
　　Around her form is flitting,
And she—how well she knows her power!—
　　She snares it in her knitting.
Here's Love that is forever new,
　　That feasts and still doth hunger—

Ah! he's eternal twenty-two
  And she a trifle younger.

Let my love, Lord, for my mate grow
  Thus god-like, to enfold her,
When she is three-score-ten or so,
  And I a trifle older.

The Perfect Solitude

When, sick at heart and weary of my kind
And of the day-long traffic, I would find
   The peace and healing touch of solitude,
I envy no lone eremite who stands,
Sealed up with silence on the desert sands,
   Where never murmurs of the world intrude.
I know a sweeter place, a holier bower
For the enshrining of the quiet hour.

Mine is a solitude that two may share,
A lamp-lit table, with an easy chair
   At either end, a friendly book for each,
And—save for clock-ticks pulsing in the room—
Sweet silence; but a silence that may bloom,
   At her will or at mine, to loving speech.
This is the dearest place, the holiest bower
For the enshrining of the quiet hour.

To a Thrush

Sing clear, O! throstle,
  Thou golden-tongued apostle
And little brown-frocked brother
  Of the loved Assisian!
Sing courage to the mother,
  Sing strength into the man,
For they, who in another May
  Trod Hope's scant wine from grapes of pain,
Have tasted in thy song today
  The bitter-sweet red lees again.
To them in whose sad May-time thou
Sang'st comfort from thy maple bough,
  To tinge the presaged dole with sweet,
O! prophet then, be prophet now
  And paraclete!

That fateful May! The pregnant vernal night
  Was throbbing with the first faint pangs of day,
The while with ordered urge toward life and light,
  Earth-atoms countless groped their destined way;
    And one full-winged to fret
    Its tender oubliette,
The warding mother-heart above it woke.
  Darkling she lay in doubt, then, sudden wise,
Whispered her husband's drowsy ear and broke
  The estranging seal of slumber from his eyes:
  "My hour is nigh: arise!"

Already, when, with arms for comfort linked,
  The lovers at an eastward window stood,
The rosy day, in cloudy swaddlings, blinked
  Through misty green new-fledged in Wister Wood.
    Breathless, upon this birth
    The still-entrancèd earth

Seemed brooding, motionless in windless space.
　　Then rose thy priestly chant, O! holy bird!
And heaven and earth were quickened with its grace;
　　Two wedded souls were moved to tears who heard,
　　　And one, unborn, was stirred!

O! Comforter, enough that from thy green
　　Hid tabernacle in the wood's recess
To those care-haunted lovers thou, unseen,
　　Shouldst send thy flame-tipped song to cheer and bless.
　　　Enough for them to hear
　　　And feel thy presence near;
And yet when he, regardful of her ease,
　　Had led her back by brightening hall and stair
To her own chamber's quietude and peace,
　　One maple-bowered window shook with rare,
　　Sweet song—and thou wert there!

Hunter of souls! the loving chase so nigh
　　Those spirits twain had never come before.
They saw the sacred flame within thine eye;
　　To them the maple's depths quick glory wore,
　　　As though God's hand had lit
　　　His altar fire in it,
And made a fane, of virgin verdure pleached,
　　Wherefrom thou might'st in numbers musical
Expound the age-sweet words thy Francis preached
　　To thee and thine, of God's benignant thrall
　　That broodeth over all.

And they, athirst for comfort, sipped thy song,
　　But drank not yet thy deeper homily.
Not yet, but when parturient pangs grew strong,
　　And from its cell the young soul struggled free—
　　　A new joy, trailing grief,
　　　A little crumpled leaf,

Blighted before it bourgeoned from the stem—
  Thou, as the fabled robin to the rood,
Wert minister of charity to them;
  And from the shadows of sad parenthood
  They heard and understood.

Makes God one soul a lure for snaring three?
  Ah! surely; so this nursling of the nest,
This teen-touched joy, ere birth anoint of thee,
  Yet bears thy chrismal music in her breast.
    Five Mays have come and sped
    Above her sunny head,
And still the happy song abides in her.
  For though on maimèd limbs the body creeps,
It doth a spirit house whose pinions stir
  Familiarly the far cerulean steeps
  Where God His mansion keeps.

So come, O! throstle,
  Thou golden-tongued apostle
And little brown-frocked brother
  Of the loved Assissian!
Sing courage to the mother,
  Sing strength into the man,
That she who in another May
  Came out of heaven, trailing care,
May never know that sometimes gray
  Earth's roof is and its cupboards bare.
To them in whose sad May-time thou
Sang'st comfort from thy maple bough,
  To tinge the presaged dole with sweet,
O! prophet then, be prophet now
  And paraclete!

251

The Journey

You are so brave, so loyal and so true!
    You bring such sunshine to the last farewell
When some far duty calls me forth from you,
    What fears consume your heart I cannot tell;
Not mine to know what prayers or teardrops pour
    From your pent heart, when you have closed the door.
But this I know: How long, how far I roam,
    My honor and my babes are safe with you
And light and sweetness shall illume our home;
    You are so brave, so true!

You are so brave, so loyal and so true,
    I should be worse than craven did I fail
To make the last long kiss I had from you
    My knightly sword and shield and triple mail.
You cannot see, through leagues of space that part,
    If passion or if peace be in my heart,
But this believe: How long, how far I roam,
    Whate'er my mind may plan or hands may do,
I would be worthy to be welcomed home
    By you, so brave, so true!

In Wintry Weather

What was the impulse wild that led us forth
    That boist'rous night,
When to the gusty wooing of the North
    The world lay white,
    And trees in icy mail
    Gave battle to the gale
      That armed them so?
What spell impelled us, dear,
To quit our ingle's cheer
    To frolic in the snow?

    O! Youth! O! wild, sweet fire
    That burnest brighter, higher,
    With strong and pure desire
      At touch of wintry weather,
    With equal flame inspire
      My love and me together!

What of the pale, gray years that are to come
    Upon us twain?
When nights tempestuous then rage 'round our home
    Will we be fain
    To pluck with fingers chill
    From Winter's heart the thrill
      That now we know?
Shall either care, my dear,
To quit our ingle's cheer
    To frolic in the snow?

    O! Age, when Youth is over,
    And we, old wife and lover,

About this hearthstone hover
  In wild and wintry weather,
With peaceful mem'ries cover
  My love and me together!

The Gates of Paradise

The gates of Paradise are double,
  And they are blue;
Blue as the skies when no clouds trouble
  Their perfect hue;
Blue as the calm face of the ocean
  When winds are still,
And sunlight only is in motion
  To work its will.
When skies are dull, the sea is lonely
  And moans or sleeps;
The quick winds or the warm sun only
  May stir its deeps.

The gates of Paradise are double,
  And they are blue;
They ope to love, but cold, gray trouble
  Will clang them to.
Lord, give me strength that I who love them
  May live aright,
And spread no tristful clouds above them
  To dim their light.
By other paths may other mortals
  Win Paradise,
But keep for me its clearest portals
  In her pure eyes.

A Child's Christmas Song

Lord, I'm just a little boy,
  Born one day like You,
And I've got a mother dear
  And a birthday, too.
But my birthday comes in spring,
  When the days are long,
And the robin in the tree
  Wakens me with song.
Since the birds are all away,
  Lord, when You are born,
Let Your angels waken me
  On Your birthday morn.

Lord, I'm just a little boy,
  Hidden in the night;
Let Your angels spy me out
  Long before it's light.
I would be the first to wake
  And the first to raise
In this quiet house of ours
  Songs of love and praise.
You shall hear me first, dear Lord,
  Blow my Christmas horn;
Let Your angels waken me
  On Your birthday morn.

To a Tenant

You found this house, dear lady, overrun
  With noisome things that wait upon decay,
  All pent within it mouldering in the gray,
Sick gloom of long disuse whose webs were spun
Through all its halls. You entered, and, the sun
  And God's air coming with you, swept away
  All ugliness and squalor, on that day
When first your life-long leasehold was begun.

You tell me now your house, this heart of mine,
  Is warm and ever-beautiful and fair,
And call me benefactor, nor divine
  How little debt you owe, how much I bear
To you who made this shabby place a shrine
  On that sweet day when first you entered there.

257

SONGS OF THE MONTHS

A Song for January

A new door opens to the fresh, sweet air,
  And one swings shut behind us.
Time still is ours! but in the darkness there
We've left a little joy, a little care,
  Whose ghosts alone go with us to remind us
How transitory pleasure is and pain,
How brief may be our faring ere we gain
One quiet nook—our own for evermore—
  And next year may not find us
With eager feet before its opening door
  When this swings shut behind us.

    But cheer! Sing cheer
    To the glad New Year!
Come, blend your voice in the chorus!
    Ho! what care we
    Where the shut doors be?
Here's an opening door before us!

A Song for February

February!
Chilly, chary
Of the vistas visionary
Through savannas blue and airy,
Where the fancy seeks to see
Promise of the days to be!
Little sun and little blue
Pierce your dull, gray mantle through;
Saddest of our months are you,
February.

Out upon you! We will sing
To another, kindlier thing,
Hoping that our song may bring
Some returning, flashing wing
Which is augural of spring
To the heavens' brightening arch.
Come, then, forward from the South
Birds with music in the mouth!
Forward! all ye sleeping seeds,
Forward! brooks among your reeds,
Violets and eglantine,
Forward! all along the line,
March!

A Song for March

Who sings of March must sing the mad,
Lone man-at-arms, the straggler clad
　In motley white and brown—
Who in the wake of Winter's flight
Turns now to caper, now to fight—
　Half hector and half clown.
One moment from a cloud-capped hill
He blares his slogan, wild and shrill;
　The next, with gusty laughter,
Outsteps the sunbeams as they dance,
And leers, and flouts with backward glance,
　The maid who follows after.
　　　　O! sing the maid,
　　　　The light-heart maid,
Who follows, follows after.

He flees her down the lengthening days;
She follows him through woodland ways,
　O'er hills and vales between,
And sets for mark of victory
On every bush and hedge and tree
　Her flag of tender green;
And when her breath hath spiced the night
With promise of the warm delight
　Of young June's love and laughter,
No other song may true hearts sing
But "Speed thy passing, March, and bring
　The maid who follows after;
　　　　The light-heart maid,
　　　　The lily maid,
Who follows, follows after."

A Song for April

(To Nancy on her fifth birthday)

"Let lovers raise
In April's praise
Songs sprung of pagan fancy,
But, oh, for me,
With eyes to see
Her very soul in Nancy,
They cannot sing
So sweet a thing
As this that April taught me—
The blessing of
The little love
Whom years ago she brought me.

So, Loveling, come! we'll wander through
Your native fields together,
And I will make my song of you
All out of April weather;
Upon a time when God's great plans
Were in his looms above us,
And all His angel-artisans,
Who cherish us and love us,
Shot shining shuttles in and out
To fashion April weather,
The little angels sat about
And sang and played together.
Oh, you shall hear the game they played,
So innocent and jolly;
They took the weavers' shreds and made
A little angel dolly!

Of blended blossoms pink and white,
    The little angels made it,
With every essence of delight
    Endowed it and arrayed it;
With soft blue bits of April skies
    And sunlight's golden flashes
They wrought the beauty of its eyes
    And of its hair and lashes.
No shred the April weavers left
    But those small angels caught it,
Inwove it in their mimic weft
    And fashioned it and wrought it.
Then God, who watched their labor, smiled
    And took it and caressed it,
And lo! it was a living child,
    For with His breath He blessed it.
So when the weavers' work was done,
    All in the bright spring weather,
Sweet April and the little one
    Came down to earth together,
And straight to our own home she flew
    And gave you to your mother!
Ay! sweet, the little child was you,
    Just Nancy and no other.

    O! who may sing
    A sweeter thing
Than this that April taught me.
    The blessing of
    The little love
Whom years ago she brought me?

A Song for May

Awake! arise! gray dreams and slumber scorning,
  For every dormer looking on the east
Is portal to the banquet hall this morning
  Where May hath called her lovers to her feast.
Lo! as it were a pledging goblet, glowing
  In her rose fingers over which do run
The golden bubbles poured to overflowing,
  Up, up, she lifts the sun!
Oh, drink with her this airy wine of spring,
That from her hands her winged breezes bring,
  Sweet philter for all hearts on earth that be!
Hark! how the birds are drunk with it and sing;
  Mark, where the flushed winds spill it on the sea,
How, lapping it, the waves go carolling;
    See how dull earth, meek flower and stately tree,
      Where'er the breezes haste it,
      Rejoice that they may taste it.
      Shall we, then, slumb'ring, waste it—
      This draught of ecstasy?
O lovers all, in this sweet wine
I pledge you and your loves and mine—
      A cup with you!
      Up! up! with you,
    And drink the May with me!

A Song for June

'Tis June! the glad time when I found thee,
　O thou, my sweet flower of love!
The dear olden glamour is 'round thee,
　The same tender sky bends above.
New beauties the summer discloses,
　But none that can rival thee now;
Not one of its fairest young roses
　Is perfect as thou.

One June brings the red rose of passion
　And marks its frail beauty decline,
But June upon June could not fashion
　The rose of a love such as thine.
Not long in the gardens of pleasure
　Are love's sweetest flowers possessed;
The love that hath leavening measure
　Of sorrow is best.
This June its new beauties discloses,
　But none that can rival thee now.
Not one of its fairest young roses
　Is perfect as thou.

A Song for July

'Tis the noon of the year.
    As a toiler, oppressed
By the labor and heat,
    Folds his hands on his breast,
Drawing strength from his dreams,
    Lo! the earth swings at rest
        In the noon of the year.

'Tis the noon of the year.
    Ere it pass to its wane,
Over full-bosomed trees,
    Over yellowing grain,
Earth, the toiler, a-drowse,
    Must revive him again
        In the noon of the year.

'Tis the noon of the year.
    Come, be one with it, sweet!
Love in idleness calls
    Through the languorous heat,
Where the dream poppies nod
    In the wind-wimpled wheat,
        In the noon of the year.

A Song for August

Since thou hast gone, I often see
    In garden closes
Faint-visioned effigies of thee
    Among the roses;
Some semblance of thy beauty's bloom,
Some savor of the sweet perfume
    That clung around thee.
But never was I fain to say
"This rose is thine" until today—
    Today I found thee.

Where Poverty in squalor lies,
    Within the city,
Where summer sears but never sighs
    With breath of pity,
How little speaks of thee; but there
Thy rose of roses, sweet and fair,
    I found this morning!
The white rose in its broken pot
An attic window's garden-plot
    I saw adorning.

Ne'er bloomed a sweeter flower of love
    In greenest valley,
Than that white rose, set high above
    The squalid alley.
If anywhere on earth thou art,
Here would'st thou hide thy mother heart
    In self-abasement;
This rose must house thy spirit mild
To cheer the little sickly child
    Behind that casement.

A Song for September

There's a death-damp in the dawn
  And a fever in the noon;
Summer's tender bloom is gone
  And her soul will follow soon.
Yet the leaves upon her trees
  And her nodding flowers fling
Benedictions down the breeze
  As they sing:

" 'Morituri salutamus,'
  But we shall not die in vain.
We shall fill your dreams with beauty
  Till the summer comes again."

There are voices in the night,
  And the calm stars overhead
Are like tapers set a-light
  In the chamber of the dead.
And the mourning katydid
  Sits and beats its strident wings,
In its leafy-covert hid,
  And it sings:

" 'Morituri salutamus,'
  But we shall not die in vain,
We shall fill your dreams with beauty
  Till the summer comes again."

A Song for October

Come, forsake your city street!
Come to God's own fields and meet
            October.
Not the lean, unkempt and brown
Counterfeit that haunts the town,
Pointing, like a thing of gloom,
At dead summer in her tomb;
Reading in each fallen leaf
Nothing but regret and grief.
Come out, where, beneath the blue,
You may frolic with the true
            October.

Call his name and mark the sound,
Opulent and full and round:
            "October."
Come, and gather from his hand
Lavish largess of the land;
Read in his prophetic eyes,
Clear as skies of paradise,
Not of summer days that died,
But of summer fructified!
Hear, O soul, his message sweet.
Come to God's own fields and meet
            October.

A Song for November

When crows croak in the leaden sky
  O'er prone grey field and spectral wood,
And all that greets thine ear and eye
  Sends eerie echoes through thy blood,
Oh, close the door and come within
Where never winter's chill may win;
      For here, my dear,
Proportioned to thy need of me
The measure of my love shall be.

When boding night-winds snarl and moan
  'Round gabled roof and frosted pane,
'Tis not our common hearth alone
  That makes the winds' forebodings vain,
But those twin sparks of fire divine
It feeds from in thy heart and mine;
      For here, my dear,
Thy need of me, my need of thee,
The measure of our love must be.

A Song for December

The earth's shroud is embossed
With gems of twinkling frost;
  The heavens snap with cold.
A wind mysterious thrills,
Above the sleeping hills,
  With music sweet and old.
The stars sang one December
  And shake with music yet;
For aye they will remember,
  Although the world forget,
The God-child's birth-cry ringing
  From out a lowly place
That set the planets singing
  In farthest fields of space.

From warm sweet depths of sleep
Where little child-hearts keep
  Their faith until the morn,
Beyond the sunset bars
To shake the farthest stars
  Another song is borne.
Their hopeful dreams ascending
  In waves of music flow,
A joyous chorus blending
  With that of long ago.
With song the night is teeming,
  But, oh, how mute we are,
Who have nor faith for dreaming
  Nor wisdom of the star!